To Herb,

A man who knows
how to Soar!

How to Soar Like An Eagle
in a World Full of Turkeys

*A Practical Guide for Personal
and Professional Achievement*

ROBERT STEVENSON

SEEKING EXCELLENCE PUBLISHING

Revised Edition Hardback – January 2006

Permissions Department
Seeking Excellence - A Robert Stevenson Corporation
3078 Woodsong Lane, Clearwater, Florida 33761.

Library of Congress Catalog Card Number 96-092715

How To Soar Like An Eagle In A World Full of Turkeys :
From Ordinary To Extraordinary
A Practical Guide To Personal and Professional Achievement
by Robert Owen Stevenson
Includes bibliographical references and index

ISBN 0-9654765-1-0

Cover Design: George Foster - Foster & Foster, Inc.

Seeking Excellence Publishing Company

Printed in the United States by Vaughan Printing – Nashville, TN

7 8 9 10

www.robertstevenson.org

This book is dedicated to
my wife Annie and my son Tyler...
who gave up a great deal of time
we could have been together
so I could have the time to write.

About The Author

Robert Stevenson's been called many things, but I'd best describe him as an idea man. Rob is a valuable resource for a great many people. He's one of those rare individuals you can call from across the country with a simple idea (*make sure you have a note pad*), and come away from the conversation with a clear direction full of creative and exciting concepts. Rob's talent has not gone unnoticed. Companies around the world are relying on him for fresh and unique perspectives on business' most crucial issues.

Rob is a proven performer. A former All-American athlete and Morehead scholar, he understands what it takes to be successful. He brings over 20 years of extensive corporate and entrepreneurial experience to this book. He's a man who knows how to deal with the risks and competition … a man who has been there. He's owned several companies, sold internationally in over 20 countries, and held positions from Salesman to Chief Executive Officer.

I feel lucky to know Robert Stevenson. I consider him a great mentor and I am thrilled that after 20 years of being in the trenches himself, turning dust into gold over and over again, his mission is now to help others reach their optimum performance level by SEEKING EXCELLENCE.

How To Soar Like An Eagle In A World Full Of Turkeys is a great place to begin unlocking your full potential. With an understanding of key concepts and philosophies that Rob so closely examines in this book, you will truly learn what it means to be an *Eagle* who can soar above all the turkeys in this world, without landing in any bird droppings. Thank you Rob for writing such an entertaining book about such a timeless issue as Turkeys. I think everyone would agree that the number and quantity of Turkeys in this world is increasing to epidemic proportions and it's about time someone offered corporate America a solution.

Susan Andreone
President, Noble Industries Inc.

Acknowledgments

There have been several people involved either directly or indirectly in the production of this book. For those indirect folks, thanks for letting me witness, learn, and watch some of life's *experiences* as a bystander. In many cases you saved me a great deal of pain.

There is no reason to thank the **Turkeys** out there because no one will admit to being one.

On a direct basis I need to start with family. My mom, dad, sister and brother have had an enormous impact on my life and will always be a part of anything I do. Their love, affection and support have always been there, which in itself, makes me a very lucky man. I was the youngest, so I was able to learn from my brother and sister. So to Mom, Dad, Joel and Sharon …thanks for all your help, support, love and laughter … thanks for being my first family.

When I finished my first draft, I knew I needed input as to the strengths and weaknesses of the book. The feedback needed to be direct, to the point, no holds barred; I'd rather be criticized by those who know me and care about me, than total strangers. Everyone I asked was happy to oblige.

I called my sister Sharon Stevenson Yates for one big reason. She has her masters in English and has been teaching English for over 20 years; who better to help edit my book than one who is so accomplished in the science of words. I also wanted her input because Sharon has been in the educational arena, not the business arena. I wanted to see if this book would help people in all walks of life, not just the corporate or sales arenas.

My brother Joel offered to help and his suggestions were invaluable. Joel has enormous entrepreneurial experience having been the CEO of an extremely successful company for over twenty years that he sold to a large publicly held entity.

More thanks must be given to my close friend and extremely successful businessman, Roger Craig. When I needed reality, fluff removal, cut-to-the-chase advice, Roger was there.

As a writer, I find that it is very easy to miss simple grammatical and typographical errors in your own compositions. You need to find someone who is a "stickler" about the written word, who has a passion for literature, an enthusiasm for reading and a fanaticism for correctness. I am fortunate to have Vivian McDonald. My sincere appreciation goes to her for the effort she put forth to insure this book "soared" grammatically.

My heartfelt thanks has to go to two special women, Lois Brown and Susan Andreone, who have been instrumental in the success of my speaking career and who played major consultative roles in the development of this book. Lois is the President of Florida Speakers Bureau, an extremely successful national bureau which provides high impact speakers, celebrities, and sports stars for meetings and conventions across the United States and the Caribbean. Susan is President of Noble Industries, a company that specializes in marketing high impact business leaders. She also has an extensive background as a sports agent and marketer. Even with their demanding schedules, not once did they not have the time for my questions. They have always been there for me; be it when I needed advice, support, criticism, editing, or prodding to complete the task at hand.

I would also like to thank my wife Annie for her patience, understanding and sacrifice. The production of a book is a labor of love for both the writer and their family. For the writer it is a commitment, a desire, a passion … but for the family it is countless hours of sacrifice … the wanting to be together but the understanding that time must be given if the book is to be written. Time that can never be given back. When I count my blessings, I count her first.

TABLE OF CONTENTS

Warning - Disclaimer

The purpose of this book is to educate as well as entertain; to try and help shorten your learning curve so you may obtain the level of success you so desire. Every effort has been made to make this book as accurate as possible. When any support material has been used I have tried to ensure that proper credit be given to the originating author. Unfortunately, I have a slight dilemma in regard to this matter. I have learned not only from my own personal experiences, but from the experiences of others as well. I have attended hundreds of seminars, listened to countless hours of audio tapes from some of the greatest trainers of this century, read innumerable books, articles, magazines, newspapers and periodicals over the last 20 years. Therefore, the possibility exists that credit may not be given where it is due, or may even be given to the wrong person. In the event that I have erred, I ask the author to forgive me. My objective has been to be completely fair with everyone; to give credit where credit was due.

The author and SEEKING · EXCELLENCE shall have neither liability nor responsibility to any person or entity with respect to any loss or damage caused, or alleged to be caused, directly or indirectly by the information contained in this book. **If you do not wish to be bound by the above, you may return this book to the publisher for a full refund.**

INTRODUCTION

I don't mean to be starting my book off on a pointed note with such a title, but:

- I wanted to get your attention.
- We do have to deal with *Turkeys* (the people kind) every day.
- *Turkeys* (the people kind) are in extreme abundance.
- The word *Turkey* does help to create a vivid image.

Let's just take a moment and compare *Turkeys* to *Eagles*.

TURKEYS ARE:

> Ugly
> Not respected
> Usually raised to be killed and eaten
> Make a stupid noise
> Have wings but yet fly poorly
> Unintelligent
> In great abundance (both the bird and people kind)
> People take offense when being referred to as a
>   *Turkey*.

EAGLES ARE:

> Far from ugly
> Very respected
> Protected from being killed much less eaten
> Quiet
> Fly with grace, power, speed and precision
> Intelligent
> Few in number (both the bird and people kind)
> People take pride in being referred to as an *Eagle*.

When I think of an *Eagle,* I have a sense of power, grace, skill and cunning, soaring high above the chaos only to enter any domain when it so chooses.

We've all heard the expressions:

> *There are a whole bunch of Indians but very few chiefs.*

> *There are many sheep but very few shepherds.*

Well, add another one to the list:

> *Too many Turkeys and not enough Eagles.*

When we think of a person as a *Turkey,* it is simple to conjure up many visual impressions. There are many different kinds of *Turkeys*; part-time *Turkeys,* full-time *Turkeys,* some *Turkeys* more offensive than other *Turkeys,* and then the special ones who must practice at it, because they are *such a Turkey*.

LET ME IDENTIFY A FEW EXAMPLES OF TURKEYS

1. A person who claims they smoked marijuana but never inhaled.

2. A person who parks in a handicapped parking space but isn't handicapped.

3. A person who parks diagonally to take up two parking spaces so they won't get their car door dinged.

4. A woman who buys an outfit from a clothing store with the sole intent to wear it to a special occasion and then return it the next day saying something is wrong with it.

5. Relatives who expect you to pay for everything when they're visiting you.

6. Friends/Associates who go out to dinner with you ... tell the waiter one check ... order twice as much as you do ... then expect to split the check.

7. People who get on moving sidewalks and stand in the center, not allowing anyone to get by, even though they hear announced instructions over the intercom to *"please stand to the right to allow other people to pass."*

8. Bosses/Associates who take credit for your work.

9. Cable television companies that keep changing channel locations.

10. Companies who install a Voice Mail system that doesn't allow you the choice of speaking to a human being.

I realize there are thousands of other examples of *Turkeys* out there that we have to deal with. In fact, in the back of the book I have listed seventy-six more examples just to help you realize that sometimes we all stumble over into the *turkey* category at one time or another. The objective now is to do a little *self analysis*: are you a *Never, Seldom, Sometimes, Often* or *Always Turkey*.

If you said **Never**, then you immediately qualify for the category and you may want to consider getting some professional help. Most of us fall in the *Seldom* to *Sometimes* category; meaning all of us can use some improvement. I hope this book will help to serve as a catalyst to get you thinking about how to improve yourself and then actively strive to do so.

Of course there are some people that the *Turkey* classification is just not strong enough for. I won't be dealing with them in this book. They are in a league all by themselves.

For those of you that have some *Turkey* examples
you would like to share in my next edition:

Please submit them to:

Seeking Excellence, Inc.
Turkey Example
info@robertstevenson.org

Please include a statement requesting submission in our next edition along with your consent releasing all rights for your original material.

CHAPTER 1

Congratulations
You Bought The Book

That's a step in the right direction, but only a step. What's scary, sad, disappointing and surprising to me is that over 85 percent of people who purchase a *personal improvement* book don't finish it. It usually has nothing to do with the book. That's just the way it is for self-help books.

Most people seem to have good intentions, but no follow-through. So do yourself a favor and decide right now that YOU WILL FINISH THIS BOOK. Make the commitment. You may want to just read a short chapter per day, but do it. Thomas Paine wrote: *"That which we obtain too easily, we esteem too lightly. It is dearness only which gives everything its value. Heaven knows how to put a proper price on its goods."*

The principles are sound. The methods are proven. The rewards are there. The choice is yours.

Don't question the agenda of the critic; just learn from it, because the end result is a better you... not a better them.

Robert Stevenson

Section I

The Mental Side of The Game

CHAPTER 2

Handling And Welcoming Change

Awhile back I was working with the Anheuser Busch corporation when one of their people, Mr. Joe Mullins, shared the following statement with me while we were discussing the subject of handling change. Joe said, *"Change is not a way of life, it is life."* Joe's ten simple, single syllable words, pretty much sum up the subject. You can complain about change, try to ignore change, fight change, resist change, not accept change; but it's going to happen.

In the computer industry they have a saying: *"If it works, it's obsolete."* They are right; especially for that industry. It has been said that the computer industry doubles in capacity every eighteen months. That means if you were comparing the automotive industry in 1982 to the computer industry growth factor, instead of driving at 55 m.p.h., we would be driving at 11,000 m.p.h. today.

We are all creatures of habit to one degree or another. Most of us like sleeping in our own bed or have a certain routine we follow when we wake up or go to sleep. If you started writing a list of what you do every day that is repetitive, I think you would be surprised at just how many things you do the same way over and over again. So when something new pops up, it usually means you'll have to learn about it and possibly alter your current daily routine. But if you will just take a moment and think about all the new things you are using right now that weren't even invented five or ten years ago, you will begin to appreciate change and the benefits of change. Fax Machines, Automatic Teller Machines, VCR's, E-Mail, Mobile Phones, Laptop Computers, Microsoft

Windows, etc., etc., etc. We now have butter that isn't butter, sugar that isn't sugar, and beer that smells like beer, tastes like beer, but it isn't beer.

Just when you think you've got it figured out, things change. You may remember one of the books business guru Tom Peters wrote entitled, *In Search Of Excellence.* This book identified the characteristics of highly successful companies, suggesting that if we followed their practices, fashioned our companies in the manner described by these *top notch* companies, we too could be successful. What may astound you is that in just three short years after the book was a best seller, 68% of the companies identified as the leaders in their industry were in deep trouble or out of business. Oh, how things do change!

And how about the demographic economic mix of our planet. Futurist Edward Barlow, Jr. explained it this way. *"By the year 2000, the world's population will increase from 5 billion to over 6 billion people, with 92% of that growth taking place outside the United States. By the year 2030, the world's population is expected to grow to 9 billion people; double what it was in 1985. America will not be the number one consumer market in the world in a very short time.* He went on to say, *"If the current demographics continue across America today, by the year 2070, the largest ethnic group in America will be hispanic, the second largest will be black, with the third largest group being white. In less than 50 years less than half of the population of the U.S. will be white. And by the year 2000, there will be more people over 50 years old than under 50 years old in America, which has never happened in our history."* Oh, how things change!

> *More U.S. workers are now employed by women-owned companies than by the entire Fortune 500.*

What guarantees success, resources or resourcefulness? If you have the resources, the strong reputation, technological riches, deep pockets, exceptionally talented people, sizable market share, worldwide distribution, do they insure success? You may want to take a moment before answering. In fact, you may want to review the following comparison list of companies before answering. If you were an investor 20 years ago, the companies on the left side were *The Players,* they had it all. But today they are no longer the bench mark in their industry. A much smaller player who only had the resourcefulness, not the resources, has beaten them out. Oh, how things do change!   *(And the following list is subject to updating)*

CBS	vs.	CNN
RCA	vs.	Sony
IBM	vs.	Compaq
Sears	vs.	Walmart

In dealing with change, I like to use the same rule I use in buying a new car or following a fad; don't be first in nor the last out. They say you should buy a car in it's second to fourth year of production. The first year a car comes out there are usually going to be some problems with them; by year two they have them corrected. After the fourth year, the car manufacturer is usually placing their research and development dollars into their new models, so you are gaining nothing by buying that model except a higher price due to inflation. I didn't purchase a laptop computer when it first came out, nor new software ... I waited a while, did my research, listened to what the critics had to say and then bought them (*the new and improved versions*). Definitely not the first in, nor the last out.

I also think you need to be very cautious when dealing with fads. Fads change; they go out of style. Now, with clothes or hairstyles you can just buy new clothes or change your hairstyle. But when we are talking about permanently altering our body, now that is something entirely different. Right now tattoos seem to be the rage along with different forms of body piercing. It's tough to change these things once they have been done. A hole in your body is a hole in your body. Pierced ears have never bothered me, but now they are piercing the same ear numerous times. We're talking lots of holes here. What happens when you want to enter corporate America; how do you hide your ears or the tattoo on your hand, neck or arm? I saw an advertisement the other day saying, *"We undo tattoos."* People got the tattoo and now want it off and the fad isn't even over yet.

This is not to say that you should be looking for everything to change. I think there is much to be said for tradition; family tradition, school tradition, religious tradition. There are certain desserts I want during the holidays. If my wife Annie doesn't make her sweet potato casserole with the brown sugar-pecan glaze on top, then my Thanksgiving and Christmas are not complete. It's hard to beat watching a sunset on a spring evening with a slight breeze in your face ... The first time you light up the fireplace in the fall ... Listening to your children laugh … The smell of home-made bread baking in the oven … Decorating the house for Christmas ... The fight song of your favorite college.

I could go on and on about the things I'd like to be the same, but when you really think about it, change occurs in all of them. I don't want the desserts all the time, nor the casserole. It takes having the day to see a sunset. Summer has got to come and go before we can have that warm fire crackling in the fireplace. It's also a pleasure to go in and see my son Tyler sleeping so calmly in his bed without a care in the world. Homemade bread is wonderful, but we would tire of it, if that is all we ate. To get to Christmas you've got to pass Halloween and Thanksgiving. And for the fight song ... well the cheerleaders outfits have changed over the last twenty years ... but leave the song alone.

I guess the point I'm trying to make is that life is an experience with everything being new, different, unusual the first time around. New experiences teach us new things and for me, that's good. But we don't have to replace everything with new.

To me, *the rule for a well balanced life* is moderation.

**Sprinkle in a little of the GOOD new,
with some tradition,
add a few memories,
and stir gently until you have a
well balanced life.**

CHAPTER 3

Stress

I can't, I just can't, I just can't handle it anymore. They, It, Them ... are driving me nuts. They want it quicker, better, faster. They want it now. Constantly changing technology. New rules, procedures, policies, people, bosses. People cutting into line. People cutting you off in traffic. Calling somebody up and getting a busy signal over and over again, and then you finally reach them and you get their voice mail.

Big stresses, little stresses, stupid stresses, fake stresses, fabricated stresses, real stresses. Stress comes in all shapes and sizes and for an abundance of reasons all of which have one thing in common: stress is bad for your health.

Stress is now the number one claim in Workman's Compensation. In terms of aging, the most significant conclusion is that the hormonal imbalance associated with stress is known to speed up the aging process. In fact gerontologists have found that the following psychosocial factors accelerate the aging process.

> Depression
> Living alone
> Job dissatisfaction
> Financial burdens
> Criticism
> Habitual or excessive worry
> Getting angry easily
> Inability to express anger

I've heard it said, *"Why worry about something you have no control over."* The words make sense, but to actually practice it is tough to accomplish; great theory, difficult execution. To me, most stress is caused personally. Poor planning, over committing yourself, not preparing properly, and lack of study are all major causes of stress. The stress is real but it is self-made.

You may want to keep a journal on this one. One recommendation I have in handling stress is to list your stresses as they occur. Explain them in detail and write out the outcome. What you will see time and time again is that you have handled problems in the past and survived, even flourished ... so you can do it again. From time to time I recommend that you just sit down and read the passages you have written. This practice will help you in dealing with current and future problems. The expression, *"Been there, done it, lived it!"* also makes much sense in stressful matters. If you can reflect back on your past experiences, from your journal or your mind, more often than not you will have handled the so-called *Crisis Situation* before.

I think it would be safe to say that stress is 80% mental and 20% actual. Oh sure, you are going to have a boss that piles things on you that you feel aren't humanly possible to accomplish in the amount of time allotted. One suggestion that might help you with that over-demanding boss is to write down a *Projects To Do List* and when they come in and give you another one, just show them the list and state the following. *"Mr. Boss, I'd be delighted to get that done for you, but where exactly does this project fall in line as far as its priority is concerned. Here is the list of what you currently have me doing, with deadline dates. Where do you want me to place this one?"* Don't be condescending or flippant with your statement, just matter-of-fact or concerned. If your boss is a *Major Turkey* and expects you to accomplish the totally impossible with no consideration to your health or family life, then you may want to consider a new job. See how well they can accomplish it without you.

> *Your only true security in life is your ability to perform.*

The first rule here is for you to be giving your best. If you are doing that and it isn't good enough, then move on. Life is just too short to be working for a *Major Turkey*.

Nike, the sports apparel manufacturer has a slogan, ***Just Do It.*** I believe for stress management there should be also be a slogan: ***Just Deal With It.*** Don't expand on it or think it will go away, ***Just Deal With It.***

If not, expect a shorter life span with more frequent episodes of poor health.

There is nothing either good or bad but thinking makes it so.

Shakespeare

CHAPTER 4

Carrying A Smile

What is most likely the first expression we ever saw; A SMILE. The moment we entered this world people were making funny faces at us, smiling at us, in great hopes that we would smile back. And when we did, boy what a wonderful reaction we would get. I love the smile of a new-born baby. It is so giving, so trusting, so happy, looking only for love.

Having a son who is only five years old, I can still recall vividly the joy I would feel in my heart when he smiled and laughed. But then the innocence wears off, the realities of life set in, and our smiles begin to fade.

Don't let it happen. In the sales arena, to be successful you need to develop *trust, confidence, and rapport*. It is a proven fact that the simple physical response of a smile is a critical tool in creating all three. If you want to be more successful and enjoy life more, then SMILE MORE. It's good for you and it's great for the people around you.

Make it a habit that before you answer the phone, smile. When you shake someone's hand, smile. In fact, make it a rule that you smile at them before they smile at you.

When you are asking someone for help, smile; it's tough to turn down a smile. If you want to change a negative state of mind, smile. Try saying the phrase, *I'm having a terrible day,* with a smile on your face. It's hard to do, and it sure doesn't seem to have the negative results as it would if you said it with a scowl on your face.

Let me say it again.

If you want to be more successful and enjoy life more,

SMILE MORE.

It's good for you and

it's great for the people around you.

CHAPTER 5

Illness ... Psychoneuroimmunology

Studies in the field of Psychoneuroimmunology have shown that the words we use can produce powerful biochemical results. Norman Cousins studied over 2,000 patients over 12 years and found that when a patient was diagnosed he became worse. Labels like Cancer, Multiple Sclerosis, and Heart Disease tended to produce panic in patients leading to helplessness and depression that actually impaired the effectiveness of their body's immune system. In other words, let's say a person was feeling ill and went to see their doctor. The doctor wasn't exactly sure what was wrong, so they had a battery of tests run. One week later, they go back to their doctor to hear the results of the tests. When the doctor explains to them what they have, they get worse. Their mind tells them, *Oh my, I've got the THIS, I should feel bad.*

In Hans Selye's book, *The Stress of Life,* he explains how adrenal exhaustion could be caused by emotional tension, such as frustration of suppressed rage. He detailed the negative effects of the negative emotions on body chemistry.

In Norman Cousin's book, *Anatomy of an Illness,* he addressed just the opposite.

> "What about positive emotions? If negative emotions produce negative chemical changes in the body, wouldn't positive emotions produce positive chemical changes? Is it possible that love, hope, faith, laughter, confidence, and the will to live have a therapeutic value?"

The answer was a resounding YES! We have a great deal to do with the healing process of our own body.

Thousands of tests have been conducted using placebo drugs with astonishing success rates. In one such study patients with ulcers were divided into two groups. Group #1 was told they were receiving a phenomenal drug that was very effective in curing ulcers. Group #2 was told that they were being given a new drug with no data available for success. They just hoped it would help. The results to the test were amazing. Group #1 had a 75% improvement rating and Group #2 had a 25% improvement rating. Both groups were given a placebo that had no chemical properties in it what-so-ever that would cure an ulcer. Just the fact that Group #1 was told they were getting a great drug made the difference. Mr. Cousins expressed it this way.

> *"Every person must accept a certain measure*
> *of responsibility for his or her own recovery*
> *from disease and disability."*

Mr. Cousins was stricken with a crippling disease. Though there was no agreement as to the diagnosis of his disease, there was however a consensus that he was suffering from a collagen illness - a disease of the connective tissue. All arthritic and rheumatic diseases are in this category. One world renowned rehabilitation clinic said that the connective tissue in his spine was disintegrating. He was told that he had one chance in five hundred for full recovery. One specialist even stated that he had not personally witnessed a recovery from his condition. In his book Mr. Cousins tells how he beat the odds utilizing the power of laughter as the main ingredient for his full recovery.

Mr. Cousins discovered that ten minutes of a genuine belly laugh had an anesthetic effect and would give him at least two hours of pain-free sleep. To make himself laugh he watched old Candid

Camera shows or Marx Brothers films. References to his illness and recovery surfaced from time to time in the general medical press. People wrote to ask him whether it was true that he *"laughed"* his way out of a crippling disease that doctors believed to be irreversible. In view of those questions he wrote the book *"Anatomy of an Illness."* I highly recommend that you read the book. Mr. Cousins describes his book as ...

> "The story of an unusual partnership between a physician and a patient and how together they were able to beat back the odds. The doctor's genius lay in helping the patient use his own powers: laughter, courage, tenacity. The patient's talent was in mobilizing his body's own natural healing resources, proving what an effective weapon the mind can be in the war against disease."

GET THIS BOOK AND READ IT!

CHAPTER 6

Handling Irate People

"The person yelling the loudest is the one losing the argument."

I have had the opportunity on several occasions to work with Busch Gardens in both their Tampa, Florida and Williamsburg, Virginia locations. To say they are a top notch organization doesn't do them justice. This is a company that is constantly Seeking Excellence in everything they do on a continuous basis.

I was asked to address their park employees on the subject of customer service. You must understand, that an organization such as Busch Gardens has to rely a great deal on part time employees who are teenagers; for many of them this could possibly be their first job. So every chance Busch gets, they try to help motivate and educate their employees in the fine art of servicing the millions of guests they entertain each year.

I interviewed several of their part-time employees to get a complete understanding of what their responsibilities were and a good idea of the customers they service every day. This is not the easiest job in the world. You have to deal with very diverse groups of guests from all walks of life. Some are wonderful people, some can be, to put it nicely, difficult. Regardless of the company, regardless of how fantastic of a job is done, there will always be customers who want to complain; Busch Gardens is no exception. You know the kind of people I am talking about: i.e., people who would walk up to a part-time sixteen year old female employee and scream at her just because it started raining. What do they think she can do about it? I know for a fact she doesn't have a weather machine.

So realizing the fact that from time to time they might have to deal with an irate customer, I prepared a little humorous "Make Believe" speech for them to deliver to the irate customer, when they were approached.

Dear Unhappy Guest:

Before we start this conversation there are a few things I would like you to know. I am an employee. I do not own this company nor do I personally know any of the owners. I am not in a management position and therefore I am not responsible for "HOW" this park is run.

I have no control over: the length of the lines for the rides, obnoxious customers, the weather, the cost of the tickets to get in, cost of the gifts, cost of the food, or the cost of anything for that matter. I don't make food selections. I have no control over where the animals scratch themselves or what they do.

Please realize I stand before you having to put up with the same weather you are and having to deal with the same guests you do. And to top it off, you are at least wearing something you chose to wear ... as for me, I have to wear this costume.

Part of my job is to help you. If you don't know where you are in the park ... I do. If you can't find a ride ... I can. If you want to know the quickest way to get to an attraction ... I know.

*I have been thoroughly trained in the art of **Customer Gorilla Warfare**. While you are speaking to me, regardless if you are yelling or even screaming at me ... I will look you in the eye and listen. I will never interrupt. I want you to get all your frustrations out. I want you to be happy. It's part of my job to help make you happy.*

I will smile throughout the entire conversation. My defense and my weapon is my smile. You may try to alter my disposition, but you can't. The best have tried and failed. Insults bounce off my smile. Abusive language just makes it wider. My smile protects me and it will help you. I want to share it with you. In fact, you can have mine, because I know how to get another one instantly.

So now that you understand this, and you have my smile, what is it I can do for you?

Now we know they can't say this to their customer. My intention was to address a very important matter from a different perspective and help them see the humor in it.

If I could help that sixteen year old teenager, standing all alone, small in stature, large in heart, face that difficult guest and keep a smile on their face; if at the start of a dialogue with an unhappy guest my little humorous speech popped into their mind and helped to shield them from the verbal attack, then I would have succeeded.

Your life is going to be full of disagreements, mistakes, confrontations and FUBAR's (*Fouled Up Beyond All Repair*). They say that the only time you don't have problems is when you're dead ... so I must really be alive. Our actions can lead to mistakes which in turn can lead to people who are NOT HAPPY. And if we've done a super job of supposedly messing things up, these people could be IRATE. The way you handle this person can have a great deal to do with your success in life.

"A person convinced against his will, is a person not convinced."

Rule 1 - Don't yell back.
        Apologize

Rule 2 - Let them talk about (*vent*) their feelings.
   Apologize

Rule 3 - Before speaking have a full understanding of what they are upset about.
   Apologize

Rule 5 - Ask them how they feel this situation should be resolved.
   Apologize

Rule 6 - Explain your position in a *Not To Prove Them Wrong Manner*.
   Apologize

Rule 7 - Throw in a few smiles during the conversation. It is mighty hard to stay upset at someone who is smiling at you.

Rule 8 - If they were wrong and you were right, don't gloat in your victory. Even though they were wrong, APOLOGIZE and tell them you understand why they got so upset.

In handling irate people the objective is not about who is winning or losing, who is right or wrong. The objective is about understanding. Stephen Covey once wrote, *"Seek first to understand, before trying to be understood."* I feel these words possess the solution to dealing with the irate. Even if the person is wrong, they still felt there was a reason for them to get upset. You should be trying to find that reason and understand it. Diffuse the cause, calm the person and establish a feeling of mutual agreement.

If your objective is to win, you have already lost.

Dealing With Jerks

Jerks are people who have graduated out of the *Turkey* categories into a class of their own. They haven't reached the Radical or Extremist categories ...yet...and they can still do *Turkey things,* but they don't care. Turkeys are usually temporary in nature whereas JERKS are full-time, bad to the bone, people .

If you intend to deal with a JERK do everything humanly possible to make everything look as if it is in their favor. You can proceed to deal with a JERK in much the same way you would an irate person, but you need to understand the difference between the two classifications.

An irate person is a person who is upset but thinks they have just cause to be upset. An irate JERK is a person who is irate, has no real reason to be irate, doesn't care what people think about them being irate, thinks only of themselves, and looks for no compromise. Their attitude can be best described as:

> ➤ *My way or the highway*
> ➤ *What's In It For Me*
> ➤ *Compromising Is Losing*
> ➤ *Sacrifice Is Sin*
> ➤ *Non-Negotiable*

JERKS are dangerous to deal with because they don't care about reasoning. In fact, anything they do care about takes a distant second to THEM.

If you apply what you learned from the *Dealing With Irate People* section of this chapter and nothing seems to work, then you are probably dealing with a JERK. In that case, try to end the situation as soon as possible, striving to minimize your losses. Deal with a JERK the same way you would deal with stepping in dog manure; clean off your shoe, remember the displeasure in doing so and **remember where you stepped.** Take the frame of mind that you didn't lose, because you were dealing with a JERK; they don't count.

JERKS are merely stepping stones on your journey towards SEEKING EXCELLENCE.

Eagles Do This
Turkeys Don't

CHAPTER 7

Criticism

If You Want To Be Successful ... Welcome Criticism

Don't you just hate criticism? I mean, think about it. It doesn't make you feel good. You tend to question the agenda of the person giving it. Is their intention to help you or look better in the eyes of others at your expense? Pure and simple, criticism is a painful experience. So why should you welcome it?

That's a good question, and unfortunately you won't like the answer. In looking back over my life, I can think of nothing worthwhile that came particularly easy. All the skills I have came at the expense of time, effort and many failures before ultimate success. A carpenter has calluses on his hands from hammering day after day. A guitar player has the same on the tips of his fingers. This should be a representation to us all that the pain will eventually leave when we have practiced enough to toughen our skin; gain the experience or learn the skill. It should also serve us to remember that the skin will soften if the practice is not maintained.

But for most professions ... salesman, manager, doctor, banker, accountant, or as for myself, a public speaker, there is no skin to toughen. There is only failure to make the sale, the inability to recognize the problem and solve it, the wrong diagnosis, poor financial advice, or miscalculation of taxes. For myself, the loss of the attention of my audience is the worst thing that can happen. All of which we would like to attribute to reasons other than our own inability.

The guitar player understands that a Band-Aid will not help to lessen the pain because he can't play the guitar with Band-Aids. He must toughen the skin by practicing day after day, just as we must do. The pain in their fingers will tell them that they are not ready yet. Oh sure, they may be able to play some songs, but can they play them all? Is there someone else out there who is better; who has practiced more than they have?

I feel you can lessen the pain of criticism by channeling it into another direction. Once we understand what we are doing wrong we are well on our way to correcting it. Regardless of the agenda of the person giving the criticism, take it at face value. Use it to your betterment even if it was given for theirs. We must remember that to get better we must learn all aspects of our profession. The hardest subject to study though is ourselves; we are prejudiced and rightfully so; if we don't think we're good, who will?

We need to appreciate that there is a time for confidence and a time for learning. We are the only person that can allow pain to enter our minds from the words that are spoken. Therefore, filter out the pain and allow only the knowledge to enter.

I wrote this piece a long time ago, after having attended a four day training program with several of my peers. I can personally attest that this is far easier to write than it is to live. During the program, I felt one of my associates was trying to make himself look good at my expense. I was first angered by what I felt to be inappropriate and incorrect criticism. I remained silent to his attack but internalized the pain and anger. A few days passed after the program and I still felt the same way. It was then I realized I needed to do something. How could I rid myself of these feelings? How could I turn this unpleasant experience to my benefit? Fueled by the anger, I began to write about criticism. Having written it, I can attest that I am beginning to allow myself to learn more about something very important to myself: me. It's about time.

The trouble with most of us

is that we would rather be

ruined with praise

than saved

with criticism.

Norman Vincent Peale

CHAPTER 8

Power Of The Brain

Let's take a look at the average brain. It's been said that the average brain can:

- **Process 30 million bits of information per second.**

- **Boasts the equivalent of 6,000 miles of wiring.**

- **Typically contains 28 billion neurons.**
  (Nerve cells designed to conduct impulses)

- **Each neuron can process 1 million bits of data.**

- **The brain has a network of over 100,000 miles of nerve fibers.**

This is the average brain. But what is scary about the brain is the fact that it is like a muscle; if you quit using it you lose it. One of the biggest mistakes you can make in life is to quit expanding your knowledge.

In school I was never really interested in learning for the sake of knowing. My interest was solely to get the grade. It wasn't until many years later that I developed my thirst for knowledge. I once had a teacher tell me that *"Knowledge is Power."* Well, she wasn't completely right. It's *the use of knowledge that's power.* I know many people who are literally brilliant, but have never reached their full potential in life because they haven't used the knowledge they possess.

What is ' holding them back? Words like obligations, responsibilities, and fear come to mind. Obligations and responsibilities I understand, but fear is unacceptable. And fear is also an overriding factor in both obligations and responsibilities. If you want to do it, you can. You don't have to take the total plunge into your dreams. Take it a step at a time. Time is the optimum word here. Take the time to prepare. The time is there. Turn off the television. Get up an hour earlier and go to bed an hour later. You'll be amazed how much time you can come up with when you put your mind to it.

The great writer Og Mandino once wrote, *"The only difference in you now and you five years from now are the people you meet and the things that you read."* Bryant Gumble once told an audience of 7,000 Realtors that; *"There are over 650,000 words in the English language. I know approximately 21,000. The average person about 15,000 and a child of 5 about 5,000. What's even scarier about these numbers is that after the age of 30 the average person learns 5 new words per annum. We quit learning."* Couple the two statements together and I think you can see what I am driving at.

We are never too old to learn. Make it your objective five days per week to do something to expand your knowledge bank. I call it a bank because of the correlation between bank and money. Expanding your knowledge and then using it will mean money in your bank.

CHAPTER 9

Establishing Anchors In Your Life

There are certain experiences in your life that forever change your life: the way you look at life, your beliefs, the way you will live your life from that moment forward. I like to refer to these events, experiences, and occurrences as **Anchors.** They help to ground me to a better life, keeping me from drifting off the path of success.

One such **Anchor** happened to me in the early 70's when I heard the great speaker Zig Ziglar talk about a boy who should have never walked, talked or weighed more than seventy pounds. His family was told time and again that the child should be institutionalized so there would be no more burden to the family. As Mr. Ziglar was sharing this story I was sitting in the audience feeling sorry for myself. I had received a rather bad injury playing football and any chance of a professional sports career was gone. I wore a back brace with steel rods in it for several years and went to numerous doctors trying to get the pain to go away.

Yes, I was feeling very sorry for myself because I had lost a dream. The young man Mr. Ziglar was speaking about did everything humanly possible just to learn to walk. I was ashamed of myself. I was a former All-American athlete who didn't appreciate what I had until it was gone and who didn't appreciate what I still had until someone else hit me right between the eyes with it. Mr. Ziglar's story of David changed my life. How dare I feel sorry for myself. I can walk, talk, see, smell, hear, taste and feel. I have no permanent paralysis, no limbs missing, no disfigurement from fire or chemicals. I hurt, and I would never play football again was all that was wrong with me. There were thousands of people who would trade places with me, but I never thought of it that way.

Mr. Ziglar's message was simple; make the most of what you have, don't dwell on what you've lost or never had. But it took the example of David to help me see the light. If you are interested in the story call Zig Ziglar's office in Dallas, Texas and they will be happy to supply you with all the details about David's story and many more for that matter. In Chapter 13 I discuss mentors; well, Mr. Ziglar was one of mine and we never met until twenty years later. His words had a profound effect on my life. The story of David will forever be one of my **Anchors.**

Another major anchor in my life was my dad. My dad is an ex-military man. One very tough individual. This is a man who volunteered for Vietnam. There were three answers my dad allowed in our household when it came to discipline: *"Yes sir, no sir, no excuse sir."* There was not a whole lot of conversation with my dad when it came to discipline. He was a powerful man at 6'4" and 240 pounds. He was an excellent athlete who at several times in his life had a scratch handicap in golf.

I received a phone call many years ago telling me to come to Atlanta as soon as possible; my father was critically ill. In all my years of living at home and up until that moment, I had never seen my father ill, other than a cold. Not once had I ever seen him sick in bed. So this came as quite the surprise.

Dad had been feeling weak and couldn't understand why, so he went to have some tests run to see what was the matter. When the doctors checked his heart they found they were dealing with a critical situation. Dad had major blockages in four arteries and was a walking time-bomb for a heart attack to occur at any moment. The doctors said they were absolutely amazed that he hadn't had a massive heart attack already.

I arrived that evening as did the rest of my family and we spent all night with dad. Before I went into his room I remember the nurse trying to prepare me for what I was about to see so I wouldn't looked shocked. Well, I'm sure I looked shocked anyway. Here was my father, a man I had never seen sick in my life lying in a hospital bed with more beepers, monitors and tubes attached to him than I could have ever possibly imagined. His color was different, his power gone, and he was straddling a fine line between life and death.

The doctors came in the next morning and said that they would be operating on him in five hours. Having spent all night in the hospital we all decided it was best for us to go freshen up and meet back at the hospital in four hours. We would do it in shifts so one of us would be with dad at all times.

I was in the room with dad alone when the doctors came early to take him down to surgery. I asked them what was going on and they said they had an operating room available and were taking him down early. I said, *"You can't do that. You told us we had five hours. You can't take my dad.* You see, I hadn't told him how much he meant to me. I hadn't told him how much I loved him. I wasn't ready for them to take my dad. I'll never forget that moment when they were rolling my dad's bed out of the room and he looked back at me and said, *"I'll be all right son, don't you worry about a thing."* He was worried how I was doing when his life was on the line.

Were those going to be his last words to me? This isn't about religion folks. I don't know if you pray to God or to a rock, but at that moment in your life you're going to pray to something. I got down on my knees and said, *"Just bring him back. It isn't fair. I haven't told him how much I love him. I haven't told him how much he means to me or how all those times he was so tough on me really helped me. Just bring him back and the woulda, shoulda, coulda's in my life will change. The people that I love will know it. I won't let it go unsaid. Just please bring him back so I can tell him."*

I was lucky, because he brought him back to me. My dad had five by-passes that day and is doing fine. In fact, just nine months later he qualified for the USGA Senior Men's Amateur Golf Championship of the United States; the top 166 amateur golfers in the U.S. over fifty-five years old. He has done it two times since his surgery.

Dad is still one tough old bird. He still likes only three answers, *yes sir, no sir, no excuse sir,* but I've added a couple of things since that day. When I speak to him on the phone I always tell him I love him and when I see him in person I kiss him and say it again. You see, I was one of the lucky ones who got their dad back. I can't tell you how many times I've told this story in one of my programs when somebody comes up later and tells me that their dad didn't make it back.

God blessed me that day. Oh, I realize my mom, sister and brother were asking for the same thing. He blessed us all. But in my private moment, alone in dad's empty hospital room, on my knees I made a promise that I will forever keep. The ones I love will always know it. My life will no longer be a woulda, shoulda, coulda life. It will have meaning, direction and a purpose and it will be centered around my family; *for success at the expense of your family is no success at all.*

My greatest **Anchor** came from my dad, and what's even better than that, is both he and my mother know it. Appreciate who you have because you will never know when you will be taken from each other. There is no question in my son or wife's mind that I love them. Why? Because I tell them several times every day. Not just by my actions but by saying the actual words. There will come a time when we won't have each other and the memory of those words will be all that's left. How sad it would be if I had never said them.

Eagles Do This
Turkeys Don't

CHAPTER 10

TCS Training

I named my company *Seeking Excellence* to help serve as a constant reminder to me to do just that; keep Seeking Excellence. Hopefully, for all of you, this will be a never ending journey; I know it will be for me.

Over the last four years, I have been involved in an extensive training program, called TCS Training. This program has helped me immensely in both my personal and business development. Many of the things that were presented to me I already knew or were obvious points of information, but were important enough to be addressed again, if I intended to better myself. I would like to share a few of these points with you so, you too, can gain from the knowledge of my instructor.

- Having a great imagination is important.
- Persistence will usually get you what you want.
- No, really doesn't mean no, it just means you need to take a different approach.
- You can get by on less sleep than you ever imagined.
- You should eat until you are full, not until your plate is empty.
- The more you read the more you learn.
- Silence is something to look forward to.
- Practice makes things easier to do.
- Being excited to see someone makes that someone feel special.
- Laughter is infectious, good for you, and good for those around you, so pass it on.
- Sometimes you have to tell people more than once what you expect of them.
- Having fun is important.

- Showing is more effective than telling.
- It's amazing what people will do for a prize or just a little praise.
- It is more effective to get people to WANT TO do something than HAVE TO.
- Failure is a major component of the learning process.
- People are going to disappoint you and not mean to.
- Being FORGIVING is a trait you MUST possess.
- Your way is not necessarily the only way to get something done.
- Saying *"Thank You"* is powerful.

Now, I realize that most of these points aren't profound. For many of us, we have heard them time and again. But, what might make them a little more special to you is if you learned something about my trainer. If you were to research the background of my trainer you would find that he hasn't studied Plato, Socrates, Demming, or Drucker; nor does he have a Ph.D. or Masters Degree. In fact, it may surprise you when you find out that he hasn't even attended school. You see TCS Training stands for *T yler C urry S tevenson Training;* actually named after the instructor of the course. That instructor happens to be my four year old son who has definitely put me through a rather rigorous training program since his birth.

In sitting down and looking back in retrospect as to what I have learned from this DYNAMO, something else became obvious to me. I started to examine what Tyler had learned over the last few years. He's learned how to speak a foreign language, crawl, walk, ride a trike, sing, draw, count, feed himself, swim, the ABC's, go to the potty(*yeah*), work the TV & VCR remote controls, turn my computer on and off (*boo*), answer the phone, swing, climb, run, say please and thank you, give love/hugs and kisses, believe, imagine, play, and laugh.

What's really scary about all of this, is that this is just a partial list of what he's learned. I then started to compare what Tyler had learned in the last few years to what I had learned; or maybe I should ask what you have learned. Mine was pale by comparison: how about you?

Sometimes people need something, someone, some event, or eye-opening experience to help them in their never ending journey towards EXCELLENCE. It may be *TCS Training* or some book you are currently reading that helps you on your journey. Just remember, don't worry about the final destination. Pay more attention to the journey and keep SEEKING EXCELLENCE.

(The previous passage dates itself every year. My son is no longer four years old, but the training has still not stopped. I hope it never does.)

Chapter 11

Attitude

*"The longer I live, the more I realize
the impact of attitude on life.
Attitude, to me, is more important than facts.*

*It is more important than the past, than education,
than money, than circumstances, than failures,
than successes, than what other people think or
say or do. It is more important than appearances,
giftedness, or skill. It will make or break
a company, a church, a home.*

*The remarkable thing is we have a choice every
day regarding the attitude we will embrace
for that day. We cannot change our past ...
we cannot change the fact that people will act a
certain way. We cannot change the inevitable.
The only thing we can do
is play on the one string we have,
and that is our attitude.*

*I am convinced that life is 10% what happens to
me and 90% how I react to it. And so it is with
you, we are in charge of our Attitudes."*

Charles Swindoll

There is a story about General Craton Abrams at the Battle of the Bulge in World War II addressing his officers concerning the serious situation they were in. I can't say that it is totally fact, or if the story has been embellished over the decades since that great battle. But I can tell you it personifies having a great attitude. This is how the story goes.

"Gentlemen we have a slight problem. We're surrounded by the Nazi's on our North, South, East, and West fronts." His men said, *"Oh no general, what does this mean?"* The General said, *"It means we can attack them in any direction. Go back and tell your men to point their guns out and shoot. They are bound to hit something."*

Now that's my kind of General. What would you rather he had said; *"It means we're all dead in about 12 hours."* That's not what I want to hear. That's not the type General I want to be with. Your attitude may be influenced by others, but it is only controlled by you. To paraphrase Mr. Swindoll; YOU ARE IN CHARGE.

> It was a chilly, overcast day when the horseman spied
> the little sparrow lying on its back
> in the middle of the road.
> Reining in his mount, he looked down and inquired of
> the little creature, *"Why are you lying upside down like
> that?"* *"I heard the sky is going to fall today,"* replied the
> bird. The horseman laughed. *"And I suppose your
> spindly little legs can hold up the sky?"*
> *"One does what one can,"* said the little sparrow.
>
> Anon.

Now that's a great attitude!

Success at the expense of your family is not true success.

Robert Stevenson

Section II

The
Mechanics
of
The Game

Chapter 12

What Are They Going To Say At Your Funeral ?

Stephen Covey, in his book *Seven Habits of Highly Effective People,* asked this question: *"What are they going to say at your funeral?"* After I first read the question, my thoughts were, who cares, I'm dead. But when I started to think about what Mr. Covey was really getting at, it changed my whole perspective. When you consider your brother or sister, minister, rabbi or priest, business associate or friend standing up to speak at your funeral, the question is not *what are they going to say* ... but more importantly ... *what do you want them to say.*

The day you make the decision as to what you want them to say is the day you start taking control of your life. The day you start to focus on what has value in your life, and the principles in which you intend to live your life by ... that is the day you start putting words in their mouths. You can live your life as an accident or as a purposeful, meaningful journey. You may not know exactly where it is that you will end up, but you can always know the manner in which you will reach that final day.

I had the opportunity a while back to work with a company several times and become friends with several of their people. I got to know one man quite well on not only a business level but a personal one as well. During our time together his father died. I had never met his father, nor had he ever spoken of him, but I wanted to do something special for him during his time of sorrow. So I sat down and wrote this poem and surprised him with it during my program where over 1,200 of his fellow associates were in the audience as well. I didn't know if he and his father were close, but I hoped that by honoring his father he would see I was honoring him.

LEGACY

I never knew this man,
I'm sad to have to say.
I never knew this man,
He's gone from us to stay.

I never knew this man,
His style, his manner, his way.
I never knew this man,
But he's in our presence this day.

You see I know his son,
A man of talent, knowledge and flair.
You see I know his son,
A man I know who cares.

You see I know his son,
A man to behold.
You see I know his son,
Made from his father's mold.

I guess I do know this man,
I'm very happy to say.
Yes I do know this man,
He's in his son today.

Robert Owen Stevenson

> # What are they going to say at your funeral?
>
> # What do you want them to say?

Set The Goals And Smell The Roses

"An unexamined life is not worth living."
Plato

If I were to give you $86,400 in cash to spend in one day, what would you do with it? What would you do if I gave you that amount of cash everyday; how would you spend it? Right now you are spending 86,400 of something everyday. Some of you are spending it wisely and some of you are just giving it away and the dreadful thing about all of this is that you can never get it back.

It takes 86,400 seconds to make up a day and most of the time **"you"** are directly responsible as to how those precious moments are being spent. By selecting the best way to utilize your time you can greatly enhance your financial, personal and physical condition.

Unfortunately we all tend to misuse this irreplaceable commodity. We all have it, we all use it and we all can never get it back. So if you can never get it back, don't you think it wise to make the most of it?

As Plato has made so perfectly clear, if our life is to be worth living, we need to examine it in detail and set out to do the best we can with the little time allotted us. We all have a limited quantity granted us, depleting at a constant rate and when we have none left everything else is of no consequence. With that in mind, there is no better time then now to examine your life, establish your goals and design your plan to reach them.

In the story *Alice In Wonderland,* Alice didn't know which road to take and when asked where she was going she didn't know that either. So the answer to her question as to which road she should take was simple: *take any road, because if you don't know where you are going than any road will take you there.*

My question to you is this. If you don't know where you are going ... how will you know when you get there? And don't get so wrapped up in your objectives that you lose appreciation for your journey.

THE MOMENT IS PRECIOUS
By Robert Hastings

Tucked away in our subconscious minds is an idyllic vision. We see ourselves on a **long ... long** trip that almost spans the continent. We're traveling by passenger train, and out the windows we drink in the passing scene of cars on nearby highways, of children waving at a crossing, of cattle grazing on a distant hillside, of smoke pouring from a power plant, of row upon row of corn and wheat, of flatlands and valleys, of mountains and rolling hillsides, of city skylines and village halls, of biting winter and blazing summer and cavorting spring and ... docile fall.

But uppermost in our minds is the ... **final destination**. On a **certain day** at a **certain hour,** we **will** pull into the station. There will be bands playing and flags waving. And once we get there **so many** wonderful dreams will come true. So many wishes will be fulfilled and ... **so many** pieces of our lives ... finally ... will be neatly fitted together ... like a completed jigsaw puzzle. How restlessly we pace the aisles, damning the minutes for loitering ... waiting ... waiting ... waiting for the station. **However**, sooner or later we must realize there is ... no ... **ONE ...** station, no place to arrive **once and for all**. The true joy of life ... **is in the trip**. The station is only a dream. It constantly outdistances us.

"When we reach the station, **that will be it**," ... we cry. Translated it means, "When I'm 18, **that will be it**. When I buy a new Mercedes Benz, **that will be it**. When I put the last kid through college, **that will be it**. When I have paid off the Mortgage, **that will be it**. When I win a promotion, **that will be it**. When I reach the age of retirement, **that will be it** ... I shall live happily ever after." Unfortunately, once we get ... "**IT**" then "**IT**" disappears. The station somehow hides itself at the end of an endless track.

"**Relish the moment**" is a good motto, especially when coupled with Psalm 118:24: "*This is the day which the Lord hath made; we will rejoice and be glad in it.*" It isn't the burdens of today that drive men mad. ... Rather ... it is **regret ... over yesterday ...** or **fear of tomorrow**... Regret and fear are twin thieves who would rob us of today.

So, stop pacing the aisles and counting the miles... Instead ... climb more mountains, eat more ice cream, go barefoot more often, swim more rivers, watch more sunsets, laugh more and cry less. Life must be lived as we go along ... The station will come ... **soon enough.**

Remember,

TODAY IS THE FIRST DAY
OF THE REST OF YOUR LIFE,
MAKE IT A PRODUCTIVE ONE!

Eagles Do This
Turkeys Don't

CHAPTER 13

Mentors

There is never enough time in your life to learn it all yourself.

If you want to speed up your learning process, you may want to select some mentors who can help you. As I have already said, there will never be enough time in your life for you to learn it all. Your mentors can be personal in nature or those you can learn from through books or audio and video tapes. Your first mentors were your parents (*other family members*). Then we move along through the educational process of school and many more mentors (*teachers*) taught us the basics of reading, writing and arithmetic.

The mentors I am really referring to though, are those people who can share their experiences (*wisdom*) with us; knowledge they have gained, through trial and error, time and study. Much of the wisdom we glean comes from living painful, time consuming experiences. Why experience the pain and waste the time if you can gain the wisdom through others sharing what they have experienced and learned already?

When my young son Tyler wanted to know what the red glow was on top of the stove, I explained. When he tried to touch it, I stopped him because I knew it would burn him. To him the glow was fascinating, and he wanted to touch the fascination not understanding the pain that would be caused by touching the burner. I knew, I had experienced the pain. I realized the outcome of his curiosity and I didn't want him to get hurt.

Now, as with all sharing of knowledge, the receiver of the information can either believe and accept the information or question and doubt the information. This is why the selection process for your mentors is very important. I don't want to waste my time questioning what is being shared. Therefore, I want to be dealing with people I know I can trust and who have no agenda to ever cause me harm; their every intention is to simply help me.

Tyler had accepted the information and didn't touch the burner, but in the back of his mind he could still be wondering just how badly it would burn him and how extensive the pain would be. He may even question me again about it and ask to see a demonstration. Not wanting him to get hurt, it would be prudent of me to design a little demonstration that would help him better accept the information I had passed on. I could possibly roll up a newspaper and just touch it to the burner and let Tyler witness the paper turn instantly into flames. Hopefully, I would be able to come up with some demonstration that would put to rest his curiosity for touching the burner.

Of course Tyler could still doubt me and decide he really wants to touch the burner to enable him to have a full understanding of what I was trying to explain. In the mentor-student relationship this is sometimes good because it helps to reinforce the true experience of your mentor and fully substantiate the value of what they are sharing with you. If Tyler had touched the burner, he would now understand the pain and have a visual reminder to live with for the rest of his life reminding him to *never touch the burner.* He would also hopefully have more faith in his mentor and next time accept what was being shared.

I don't mean to get elementary on you by using the example of my son and the burner, but the simplicity of the example I feel cuts to the core of the mentor-student relationship regardless of the advice being shared. Experience usually comes with time, but there are ways to speed up the process, so in short:

⮑ Find yourself a couple of successful people who would be willing to help you.
⮑ Make sure they have no reason to mislead you.
⮑ Ask good questions.
⮑ Listen to what they have to say.
⮑ Try and understand the *"why"* behind their answer.
⮑ Be appreciative of their time — don't waste it.

> AND READ ... Many brilliant minds have shared their wisdom in the books they have written. It's your job to study. I would recommend a minimum of thirty minutes of uninterrupted reading every day. I'm not talking about entertainment reading ... I'm talking educational reading.

CHAPTER 14

Send Cards

I've asked the question countless times in my programs; *how many cars do you think a great car salesperson could sell in one year? Would one a day be a lot? So with 220 working days that would be 220 cars sold in one year. Is that a lot?* Many people think that is incredible, but sometimes I might have to double that number. I have never taken it any higher than 440 cars. The only problem with that number is it isn't even half of what Joe Girard averaged for twelve years, selling Chevrolets on a non-fleet sales basis. Before leaving the car dealership he sold over 13,000 cars.

Joe Girard was in the *Guinness Book of Records* as the world's greatest salesman for twelve consecutive years. He still holds the all-time record for selling more people retail on a big ticket item … an average of six sales per day!

In His book *How To Sell Anything To Anybody* Joe explains how he built a solid rapport with his customers by staying in constant touch with them by mail. He wanted to make sure that after the sale, his customers would never forget him. So every month of the year his customers received a card from him. It would arrive in a plain envelope, and he would vary the size and color of the envelope so nobody would know it was from him. Inside the envelope was a card with the message inscribed on it, *I Like You.* Then there would be a different message inscribed on the inside of every card; for January it would have *"Happy New Year from Joe Girard,"* March was *"Happy St. Patrick's Day,"* and so on for every month of the year.

He would send out over 14,000 cards per month. That's 168,000 a year. When you multiply that by the cost of a first-class letter, you will see that he was spending more on postage than the average car salesperson makes a year. Was it worth it? Joe said that the letters were greatly responsible for sixty-five percent of his sales that were repeat business.

In Gail Sheeby's book, **Character,** she pointed out how former President George Bush spent two hours every night writing notes to friends, family, partners, and acquaintances. She said, *"Closeness requires action."* Boy is she right!

There is a really simple way to look at this:

Out of Sight — Out of Mind

CHAPTER 15

Endearment

Be Different, Be Memorable

I once heard it said, *"People don't care how much you know, until they know how much you care."* That statement should be the foundation for every organization. If a company truly cares about their customer more than they do about making the sale, they have a far better chance for success than the company who has the mind set of *Sell, Sell, Sell.*

From the initial contact I have with any person I start an account card on them. I want to get as much information as possible about them and I want to be able to remember what was said, so I write it down. ***The palest ink is far better than the greatest memory***. I have an abbreviation system for some things, especially when I can't reach them and have to leave a message.   i.e.:

NILM -   Not In Left Message.
OPLM -   On Phone Left Message

I think it is important to write down every time you contacted the person to keep a pulse on the possibility of them not wanting to speak to you. This is critical for salespeople. I had a rule: if I saw five entrees on an account card where I had left a message, but my client/prospect never called back, I instantly knew I had a problem.

I would then take a different approach to try and get them to call me back. I might send them a seven foot by five foot telegram expressing the importance of our speaking, or a personalized article; something that would get their attention.

I also made it a point to obtain their birth date. If you were to think back on how many birthday cards you received last year, you could probably remember who sent every one. So if I sent you a card, my card would stand out to you. People like being remembered on their birthday. I send out lots of birthday cards. My computer tells me the 25th of every month prior to the month the cards are to go out, who is to get a birthday card. I also personally hand write a message on every card.

Joe Girard showed us how his card campaign was a critical element in his success formula; I just happened to add one more card to the formula. Joe sent out cards; I send out a newsletter designed to brighten the day of my clients and potential clients. Whatever vehicle you are thinking about using, remember to keep it short and to the point.

You may also want to consider gathering other information about your client/prospect on your account card.   i.e.:

Married	Yes	No	Name
Children	Yes	No	Name(s)
Education			
Member of what groups?			
Military background			
Religion			
Favorite foods			
Favorite desserts			
Favorite color			
Hobbies			
Favorite charities			

Harvey Mackay in his book *Swim With The Sharks Without Being Eaten Alive* points out how he requires his salespeople to strive to get sixty-six points of information on their clients. Some of you might think that is a little overkill, but for Mackay's company it works. His salespeople average twice the industry average in compensation.

Knowing what is important to people is an excellent way to build rapport. If I find an interesting article written about the University of Alabama, I go to my computer and pull up every major client who went to the University of Alabama and send them a copy of the article. I don't ask for any business. I don't try to make an appointment. I just hope they enjoyed the article. I hope they read it, and then think, *"that sure was nice of Rob to send this to me."* Remember, ***People don't care how much you know until they know how much you care.***

Some of you may be wondering how in the world can I pull up on my computer who went to the University of Alabama. It really is very simple. I have an account management system on my computer that allows me to customize my accounts in the manner I feel is important. Name, title, company name, address, phone number, and fax number is standard information, but I can go into the system and assign other field categories that are of significance to me. It is a very inexpensive software program and well worth the investment.

I am however redundant in my record keeping. I have been keeping account information on my clients/prospects for years, long before simplified account management software programs were ever around. At one point in my career I had over 350 accounts worldwide and it was very important that I did not forget anything about those clients. I started putting my account cards in a notebook, with dividers separating each account card. I also put letters they sent to me in the book, along with a copy of anything I ever sent to them. If you walked into my office today you would see twenty-one three inch notebooks within arms reach of my desk. Even though I have all the account information on computer now, I still keep the notebooks. I guess old habits are hard to break, plus computers can crash … my notebooks never have.

If I call someone or they call me, I just pull down the notebook which has that account card in it and start taking notes during the call. I have maintained this system because it allows me to keep everything that has ever happened with that client right in front of me. If any questions arise while we are on the phone, I have the entire history of that account right in front of me.

If I call a client and they tell me that they can't talk because their son Billy just broke his ankle, I write it in my book. Two things will then happen. First of all I will send a card to my client expressing my concern over his son's ankle and secondly, when I call him the next time, the first words out of my mouth will be, *"How's Billy's ankle?"* With over 350 clients, it is very possible that's Billy's ankle could have slipped my mind the next time we spoke, had I not written it down on my account card.

When I say account card, please don't take that to mean I have only one page of information on each account. When I say account card, I mean the initial sheet that has all the standard information and then all the pages of notes I have taken on phone calls and follow-up. I just use a lined white sheet of paper after the standard form to keep all the other information. If I call them, I write it down. If I send out a letter, I write it down and keep a copy of the letter.

I send out jokes, bumper stickers, poems, or anything I feel would be of interest to my client. I never include anything that has to do with selling when I send out an ENDEARMENT message. You need to do this because you care.

So send out those cards, letters, jokes, poems, birthday greetings, and make your client feel special. If it wasn't for them, you wouldn't have a job, so that makes them pretty special.

Now it isn't necessary that you do any of these things. You can choose to be just like the majority of all the other average people out there. I like being different, I like being memorable ... and so do my clients.

Remember,

People don't care how much you know until they know how much you care.

Anon.

CHAPTER 16

Health & Fitness

Exercise

The physical condition of your body is of critical importance in everything I talk about in this book. Neither your mind nor your body can function, perform, or produce the results you are looking for without proper physical fitness.

It has been proven that the aging process can be slowed down considerably through proper exercise. Researchers at Tufts University have discovered that the symptoms of biological aging can be improved through increased activity. Scientists William Evans and Brian Rosenberg wrote a book entitled *Biomakers,* where they recorded their findings on this subject. Dr. Deepak Chopra's brilliant book, *Ageless Body, Timeless Mind,* speaks of "the quantum alternative to growing old." *(Chopra's book contains the findings of Evans & Rosenburg along with other amazing information concerning the slowing down of our aging process ... I highly recommend his book)*

One example Chopra shares was that of the study conducted by Evans & Rosenberg on twelve men between the ages of sixty to seventy-two, who were put on a regular supervised weight-training program of three times per week for three months. At the end of the experiment, the men's strength had increased dramatically, the size of their quadriceps had more than doubled, and their hamstrings had more than tripled. By the end of the experiment, these older men could lift heavier boxes than could the twenty-five-year-olds working in the laboratory.

Gerontologists from Tufts University selected the frailest residents from a nursing home and started them on a weight training program. Within eight weeks, wasted muscles had come back by 300 percent, coordination and balance had improved, and an overall sense of active life returned. What makes the study so amazing is that the youngest participant in the group was eighty-seven and the oldest was ninety-six.

UCLA researchers and the Surgeon General have estimated that two-thirds of the illnesses suffered in old age are preventable. At the top of their list of causes for those who died earliest were 1) People who had sedentary lifestyles. 2) People who smoked.

Why people decide to quit exercising is beyond me. *You can't do that, you're too old,* is an old wives tale. In Chopra's book he stated: *"By adopting a healthy lifestyle, you can delay the symptoms of aging by as much as thirty years."* Let's just say for debate purposes that Dr. Chopra's number is incorrect; he's off by 70%. I can't think of anyone who would complain about adding seven more years to their lifespan.

If it has been several years since you exercised, go to your doctor and make sure everything is okay before you start anything. Once you have your doctor's approval, then start off slow. Let's don't go out there and make ourselves so sore after we exercise the first time that we aren't going to want to do it again. Start out with a walk around the block and build from there.

Ms. Mavis Lindgren was a sixty-two year old mother of three when she decided to take up jogging. Eight years later she ran her first marathon. At the age of eighty-six she ran in the New York Marathon; her 65th marathon in sixteen years. When she took up jogging at the age of sixty-two, her first jog did not last a block. She started off slow, set her goals and then *JUST DID IT.*

Walter M. Bortz, a senior physician at Stanford University, who is a specialist in aging coined the term *disuse syndrome* to describe how lack of attention to our body's basic requirements, especially the need for physical activity, can destroy health and lead to accelerated premature aging. It is a well-established fact in physiology that any part of the body that isn't used will begin to atrophy and wither away.

There is a very simple rule in exercise. *You either use it or lose it.* Again, it's your choice.

Sleep

Sleep deprivation is a major cause for people getting sick today. It is hard for a run down body to fight off a virus. A well-rested immune system has a far better chance of fighting off a virus than a weakened one; and one of the quickest ways to weaken your immune system is to deprive yourself of enough sleep.

The rule for enough sleep varies from person to person. Many folks can get by on a great deal less sleep than others, but the key words here are *get by*. You might be able to do it, to *get by* on five hours sleep, but have you weakened your system to where you are more prone to getting sick?

Most doctors would suggest seven to eight hours of sleep per night. Just remember that your health, alertness of mind, and responsiveness to conditions around you all have a great deal to do with the amount of sleep you get; or should I say, the amount of sleep you don't get.

Proper Weight

If you gain just one pound per year, in twenty years you're going to wonder what happened. There was no major change in your appearance from year to year, but cumulatively the effect is drastic.

I get a real kick out of all these people spending so much money on special diets. I thought about writing a diet book, once. It wouldn't be very long. In fact, it's so short, I think I'll share it with you.

Title:

It's All A Matter of Desire

Chapter 1:

I am not talking about overweight people who have eating disorders, medical problems, etc. who need to be under a doctors care ... but for the rest of you ... for those of you who say you just can't lose weight, I disagree. It all comes down to a question of desire. It is unfortunate that ninety-five percent of the people who go on diets gain the weight back. The fact that is important is the diet did work; they lost the weight and then at some point in time fell right back into their old habits and gained it back. Some of you may be disappointed to hear the ninety-five percent number, but that is not the place to dwell. It's the five percent that's exciting ... they did it. If we have one million people going on diets, that equates to 50,000 people who make it and stay. To me 50,000 people is a lot of folks. And if they can do it, so can you. The other people just go back to the way they use to be, awaiting their next attempt. **It's all a matter of desire.**

Chapter 2:

Let's see if we can make this simple. If you eat more calories than your body burns you will gain weight. If you eat less calories than your body burns you will lose weight. If you exercise your body will burn more calories. So, if you want to lose weight you can either eat less, exercise more, or do both, as long as it all adds up to burning more calories than you take in.

Chapter 3:

Don't try and lose the weight too fast. It took you a long time gaining it, so don't try and kill yourself taking it off. If you over compensate, you will eventually fall right back into the same pattern and gain the weight back.

Chapter 4:

Quit lying to yourself. The problem with your weight problem is you. Start eliminating the cheap calories. Start paying close attention to what goes into your mouth; be mindful of fat grams and calories. Don't eat late at night. Get control of your life. Make the time to take care of the most important thing you possess, your health. Keep telling yourself, *"If 50,000 people can do it, so can I." It's all a matter of desire.*

I told you it would be a short book. Now, I realize there are many of you out there that aren't fond of my approach; you may think I am not caring or considerate about this issue. How I feel about this issue is not important; getting you in shape so you can live a long, prosperous, enjoyable life is the issue. If you are overweight, one of your problems could be that people have been too considerate of your problem. If you are overweight and don't want to be, only you can do something about it. If you want to change the way you look then get mad at yourself. Make the commitment to do something about it and then DO IT! *It's All A Matter of Desire.*

Let's get something straight here before we go any further. I am not saying being overweight is bad, ugly, or wrong. I am saying that it isn't good for your health. Being too skinny is not good for your health either. Go to your doctor and find out where your ideal weight should be and then do what is necessary to get there.

The incidence of heart attacks has doubled in The United States every two decades since 1900. Dr. Paul Dudley White, an eminent cardiologist believed the epidemic was due to primarily two changes: 1) The enormous acceleration in our everyday pace of life *(stress)* and 2) The enrichment of our diet. *(enrichment meaning the adding of more fat in our diet)*

If you were to plot the incidence of heart attacks, arteriosclerosis, breast cancer, and colon cancer in countries of the world *(who has the most to who has the least)* and compare that list to a list of countries of the world who consume the most milk, red meat, eggs and cheese, you will see that the same distribution occurs. This is telling us that the societies with the richest diets have catastrophic rates of heart attacks, hardening of the arteries, and cancer.

Obesity is rising in most industrial nations. Epidemiologists have settled on a consistent category for measuring the disorder; BMI *(Body Mass Index)*. To calculate your BMI use the following equation.

$$\textbf{BMI} = \frac{w \text{ (pounds divided by 2.2)}}{h^2 \text{ } h \text{ is height in meters}}$$

w is weight in kilograms
h is height in meters
(inches divided by 39.4)

The National Institute of Health and the American Health Foundation issued new guidelines in 1995 defining healthy weight as a BMI of below 25. According to a recent report of the Institute of Medicine, 59 percent of American adults exceed that threshold. Your personal risk of developing heart disease, cancer, type II diabetes, high blood pressure, degenerative arthritis and/or gallstones increases significantly at BMI's of 25 or higher.

According to the New England Journal of Medicine the probability of a person developing heart disease with a 27-29 BMI is 210% more than a person who has a BMI of below 19. If their BMI is 29-32 it increases to 360%. And if their BMI is 32-35 it increases to 480%. In layman's terms ... excessive weight can kill you.

I am no doctor, nor do I attest to being some sort of guru in the nutritional field. Am I a saint when it comes to not letting any BAD foods enter my body? Heavens NO; but I do pay attention to the cheap calories. I pay attention to the foods high in fat. I don't live on salads, nor do I over-indulge in desserts. I do however exercise regularly and if I pick up a few pounds I cut back on what I eat.

I have one simple measuring tool for me; I will not purchase a larger pair of pants. Every day when I put on a pair of trousers I just found out if I would be eating less that day. Tight pants means one of two things to me; either cut back on the food or increase my exercise (or both). It does not, nor will it ever allow me to purchase a larger pair of pants. Some of you use the weight scales, I just happen to use a pair of pants. There have been times that my pants have been very uncomfortable, and that is okay. That uncomfortable feeling is a constant reminder to me to eat less and pay close attention to what I do eat. A little common sense, a mirror and a pair of pants are my key ingredients to staying slim.

Smoking

Don't do it ... Enough said

Let me see if I can explain how I really feel. Smoking:

▶ Gives you bad breath
▶ Dulls your taste buds
▶ Turns your teeth yellow
▶ Discolors skin on the fingers that hold the cigarette
▶ Makes your hair, clothes, house, car, office smell bad
▶ Is addictive
▶ The smoke offends most non-smokers
▶ Is expensive
▶ Causes excessive facial wrinkles
▶ Has been proven to cause cancer ... smoking can kill you

And as far as smokeless tobacco is concerned, that is even worse.

With our life span as short as it already is, why in the world would you want to shorten it even further. And for those of you who are smokers, please stop. You have friends and loved ones who care a great deal about you and want you around as long as possible. *So don't do it ... Now, enough said.*

Drinking

There have been thousands of wonderful people who have been killed by drunk drivers. Those drunk drivers may be sorry for what they did, but that will never bring those wonderful people back; **being drunk can never be an excuse for your actions.**

I feel the answer to drinking is a simple one. Extreme moderation with no form of driving. And since we're on the subject of drinking we might as well hit upon the subject of drugs. Let me see if I can make this perfectly clear; doing drugs is stupid. Why?

- ☐ It's expensive
- ☐ It's illegal; if caught you go to jail and it stays on your records
- ☐ It can cause you to do things you would never do sober
- ☐ It can kill you
- ☐ It can cause you to kill

With the exception of illegal, these points apply to drinking as well. I heard a person one time talk about "taking cocaine." He explained that after the first initial high, you were always chasing it. He then went on to explain that once hooked it would posses you. And he left us with this description of what's it like taking cocaine after getting hooked. He said; *"take a hundred dollar bill, roll it up and then burn it. After that, take a piece of sand-paper and stick it up your nose and twist it around until your nose bleeds. That's what it's like taking cocaine once you've been hooked. So if you still want to try it, give me the hundred and I'll give you the sand-paper."*

I just look at all the great athletes whose lives have been ruined by taking illegal drugs. I have never looked upon anyone who took drugs as being cool. I always saw them as people who were weak; *who needed a drug* to make them feel better, complete, be part of the *in-crowd*, powerful, or high.

But, just because you took drugs or became an alcoholic doesn't mean that your life is forever ruined. I had a man who worked for me for years as the foreman in charge of over 100 people, who was a reformed alcoholic. I'll never forget him telling me in the interviewing process that he was an alcoholic. He looked me straight in the eye and said with no hesitation, *"Mr. Stevenson, I want you to know that I am an alcoholic."* That statement came as quite a shock to me, but was also one of the reasons why I hired him. I felt it took real guts to tell me that. After I hired him I found him to be a fantastic person and an exceptional worker; who also became my friend. Sometimes you get lucky I guess. He was lucky to get the job and I was lucky to have him.

He had looked upon his past with sorrow and regret, but more importantly, with honesty. He once told me that he had a lot of excuses for getting drunk, all of which, never added up to one good reason.

Conclusion

To put the need for better *Exercise, Sleeping, Eating and Drinking Habits* into a more tangible account let me share with you a study conducted by a Southern California research team headed by Nadia Belloc and Lester Breslow, now the dean of public health at UCLA, following the aging patterns of people in Alameda County, California.

◆ 23 page lifestyle questionnaire
◆ 7,000 subjects in the study
◆ 5 ½ year study
◆ In 5 ½ years 371 of the subjects died

Looking back over the original responses of their questionnaire, researchers found that the most important features of those who survived was not their:

❖ Income
❖ Physical Condition
❖ Genetic Inheritance

What stood out were the following seven points.

❶ Sleeping seven to eight hours per night

❷ Eating breakfast almost every day

❸ Not eating between meals

❹ Normal weight — i.e., not more than 5 percent underweight, and no more than 10 to 20 percent overweight. *(the lower number was for women, the higher number was for men)*

❺ Regular physical activity — i.e., engaging often in active sports, long walks, gardening, or other exercise

❻ Moderate drinking — i.e., taking no more than two alcoholic drinks per day

❼ Never smoking cigarettes

Analyzing the statistics, they found that a forty-five year old man who observed from zero to three healthy habits could expect on average to live another 21.6 years, while someone who followed six or seven good habits could expect to live thirty-three more years. Probably even more astounding than this was the fact concerning overall health. A person in their late middle age (55 to 64) who practiced all seven good habits was found to be as healthy as a young adult (age 25 to 34) who followed only one or two. The seven factors for living longer are all controlled by you and you alone. ***If it is to be, it's up to me.***

CHAPTER 17

Proper Dressing / Grooming

A long time ago, I was asked to put together some guidelines for a company that wanted to address the importance of proper dressing/grooming for their sales team. Having read back over the piece, I felt it appropriate for any profession and therefore, decided to share it with you.

The Brass Tacks of Selling

You never get a second chance to make a GOOD first impression!

People want to do business with people who look successful.
So before you even walk out the door you need to look the part.
This is a requirement if you want to be successful.

APPEARANCE

Current clothing
Looking stylish
Looking fresh - knowing what fabrics to buy your clothes in

HANDS

Male - Make them look like the hands of a doctor, well-kept fingernails, trimmed evenly and clean. Your hands are a sales tool make them look as such.

Female - You may want to consider having your fingernails professionally done (*or at least look as if they were*). Nails that are done this way add an air of sophistication to any woman and, as with your male counterpart, will help in your sales presentation.

SCENT

Female - Spend money on one of the top colognes in the industry. Go to a major department store fragrance counter and talk to the salesperson about what is a light professional scent.

Male - The same as with females.

Don't let the scent be overpowering.
It should be noticed when people get close to you,
not when you walk into the room.

HAIR

Look in magazines and find out what are some of the current styles. Many people have the same hair style they had 5, 10, 15 years ago. They are in a rut and never change. Whatever the style, make sure it is clean and kept looking. Dandruff is totally unacceptable; if you can't get rid of it yourself, go see a doctor.

SHOES

Polished ... a necessity. Wear current styles.

BRIEFCASE

Nice looking and well organized and with all the necessary sales tools, agreements (contracts) in it.

PEN

A professional writing instrument is critical and is also a sales tool.

BREATH

How do you like talking to someone who has bad breath? Don't you want to end the conversation quickly so you don't have to put up with the odor? If this is the case, make sure you don't have bad breath. A simple trick I have learned that helps is to buy Tic Tacs and place one in your mouth between your cheek and lower gum towards the back. The mint will stay there and not fly out while you are talking and insure that your breath is fresh. This also helps a great deal when you have a cold and are taking medication that dries you up ... the mint will insure you don't get dry mouth.

SMOKING *(refer Chapter 16)*

This is a habit that is becoming less and less acceptable in our society. I realize it is an addiction and a very hard habit to break, therefore, if you must smoke, do so before you go into a meeting and then use a breath freshener. I do not feel it is acceptable to ask someone if you may smoke in their office, home, car, etc. You are there to do a job, not smoke, therefore, smoke on your own time, away from clients. You may also want to reconsider not smoking in your car if you use it for transporting clients. The odor of your car could be offensive to potential clients and cost you a sale.

CLOTHING

When buying clothes remember you need to look as good in the afternoon as you did in the morning so fabric selection is critical. I call it the *crunch test*. Before buying a business suit (outfit) take the garment in your hand and squeeze it *(crunch)* for 5 seconds and then let it go. If the garment looks all wrinkled and doesn't bounce back into it's original shape in a few seconds then don't buy it. Simple Rule: If it wrinkles easily on the sales rack it will wrinkle easily on you too. To me a wrinkled look is not a successful look. Why people buy linen amazes me. I know it looks good on the rack but it looks terrible on you just as soon as you sit down. I guess if you are having a party and are planning not to sit down, bend your elbows (for long-sleeve linen shirts), lean up against something, or hug anyone, then linen is the fabric for you.

I would also try and wear colors in which it is hard to detect perspiration spots. White shirts are a winner in this category along with dark suits. Remember the old negotiating adage;

Never let them see you sweat.

These are just a few of the things you need to consider. You are trying to accomplish an overall look of success. Make sure you have that look all day long. Look at what other successful people are wearing that have a look you want, and copy it. Ask them where they bought what they are wearing. Don't hesitate to ask, this is a compliment to them and they will be happy to tell you. Find a good clothing store and frequent it. Try and catch the sales and concentrate on expanding your wardrobe through mixing and matching.

... Remember ...

You want the way you look to demand Respect.
People like to deal with people who are successful
and you need to look the part.
You haven't even walked out the door yet.
This is a prerequisite before starting.
Looking the part.

Eagles Do This
Turkeys Don't

CHAPTER 18

Communication

The ability to communicate is the single most important skill determining your success in life.

Bert Decker

To communicate effectively you must create three things.

Trust, Confidence, Rapport

If I have confidence in you, if I trust you then, I will believe you. It's tough to have one without the others. What is the language of trust?

✦ Do they talk too fast
✦ Does their voice quiver
✦ Does their voice project authority
✦ Do their hands shake
✦ Do they look you straight in the eyes
✦ Is their handshake firm
✦ Are they nervous
✦ Do their eyes dart back and forth

Communication is done on three levels, Auditory, Visual, and Kinesthetic. The most prominent of these three is Visual. In fact, when speaking to someone face-to-face your ability to communicate comes across through the *words* you use, the *tonality* of your voice and *visual* imagine you convey. If you were to add up the three elements to equal 100 percent: Verbal accounts for 7%, Tonality accounts for 38% with Visual accounting for 55%.

The power of Visual is incredible. The believability of your message has a great deal more to do with the way you look, the energy you possess, the enthusiasm in which you present your message as compared to that of just the words you speak. People look for your conviction in your eyes, your mannerisms and your gestures.

The ability to communicate falls into eight major categories:

- Eye Communication
- Posture and Movement
- Dress and Appearance
- Gestures and Smile
- Voice and Vocal Tonality
- Words and Nonwords
- Listener Involvement
- Humor

REMEMBER:
*You never get a second chance to make a **good** first impression.*

The key word here is GOOD. You are going to make an impression the first time; just what kind of impression you make is entirely up to you.

■ Eye Communication - if your eyes are darting back and forth you look *Shifty*. You need to look them straight in the eyes; this helps to convey confidence.

■ Posture and movement - stand tall, erect, with shoulders back. Move with precision, purpose and grace. It is tough to have confidence in some slouched over, slow moving, timid person.

■ Dress and Appearance - refer to Chapter 17

■ Gestures and Smile - when speaking add emphasis to what you say with your hands. In large groups use larger gestures, in small groups tone them down. In one-on-one situations keep them tight and into your body. But by all means smile. The first thing we ever learn to trust is the SMILE coming from our parents. The simple act of smiling is one of the greatest confidence builders you have. It attacks the subconscious of the person you are speaking to, helping to break down the barriers of distrust and concern.

■ Voice and Vocal Tonality - the way you sound to you and the way you sound to me are different. Go get a video camera or tape recorder and record you speaking on the phone or in casual conversation. When you play it back, what you hear is what they hear. You may not like what you hear. It may be twangy, or shrill, or too fast, or too slow ... but it's you.

The great thing about all of this is that it can be changed through practice. Ask some friends or family members what they like and dislike about the way you talk. Don't take umbrage with what they say. Don't try and defend how you speak. You are looking for some constructive criticism, so shut-up and take notes.

The expert communicator pays attention to the way you speak and tries to mirror your speech patterns. If you speak fast, they will too. If you speak slowly, they will adjust their speech patterns to match yours. They know that one sure way to develop rapport with an individual is to fall in line with the manner in which they are being addressed.

If you have any interest in studying this in more depth, then go to your local library or book store and get books on the subject of Neuro-Linguistic Programming and Conditioning. It is a fascinating science discovered in the 70's by John Grinder, one of the most prominent linguists in the world, and Richard Bandler, a mathematician, Gestalt therapist and computer expert. Read anything they have written on the subject. There are several books on the subject that I would also recommend.

The Power of Business Rapport	Dr. Michael Brooks
Instant Rapport	Dr. Michael Brooks
Unlimited Power	Anthony Robbins

The Nightingale-Conant Corporation in Chicago is always coming out with audio and video tape series on the subject; all of which are quality programs.

■ Words and Nonwords - if the words you say only account for 7 percent of your overall ability to communicate, then I would suggest you select those words wisely. That doesn't mean that to sound impressive you need to sprinkle your vocabulary with four syllable words nor does it mean to speak on a sixth grade level.

As I said in Chapter 8, which I feel is worth repeating, there are over 650,000 words in the English language ... the average person knows about 15,000 words, and a child of five knows about 5,000 words. What is really scary about this is that after we turn 30 years old, we average learning about 5 new words per annum; we quit learning. Keep studying, expanding your knowledge, and refining your vocabulary. And remember, it is not just what you say but how you say it. Eyes, mouth, hands, gestures, and mannerisms can convey a message long before any words are spoken. Your body language can kill or make any communication.

■ Listener Involvement - if you want to get your point across then elicit listener involvement. Get them involved in the conversation. Get them talking and listen to what they have to say. In the business arenas of negotiations and sales as well as in just developing rapport with people or making friends, there is a simple rule applied to be a successful communicator...

Listen twice as much as you speak.

The good Lord gave us some help in remembering this rule by giving us two ears and one mouth; so listen twice as much as you speak.

You will never be able to learn anything when you are the one who is doing all the talking. By asking good questions, and then shutting up and listening, you have an excellent chance to learn something. People are more accepting of you when they are doing most of the talking.

An excellent conversationalist / communicator is a person who gets the other person talking. If you want to see one in action watch the television show *Larry King Live*. Get two stop watches and time every time the guest speaks and every time Mr. King speaks; you'll see a perfect example of the rule in action.

■ Humor - Victor Borge said: *Laughter is the shortest distance between two people.* By incorporating humor into your repertoire you will greatly enhance your ability to communicate. But there is one rule that needs to be established right up front with this advice.

1. Humor at the expense of someone else is not acceptable.

You should also be careful with religious, ethnic, or gender jokes. You might think you really know someone well and then be in for a big surprise when it's too late; the damage is already done, your stupid joke has already been spoken.

Oh, and for you good old boys who think that telling sexist or dirty jokes in front of your female associates is not offensive, think again.

What do you need for success in your career? Professor Thomas W. Harrell of the Stanford Graduate School of Business researched that question during a twenty year longitudinal study. Professor Harrell concluded that while there was no guarantee for success, there were three qualities that consistently appeared to have a positive influence on the professional careers of those studied:

❶ An outgoing, ascendant personality.
❷ A desire to persuade, to talk, and work with people.
❸ A need for power.

The "ability to communicate" has extreme bearing on the first two.

> *The man who can think*
> *and does not know how*
> *to express what he thinks*
> *is at the same level of him*
> *who cannot think.*
>
> **Pericles**

Greatest Fears

1. Public Speaking	41%
2. Heights	32%
3. Insect & Bugs	22%
4. Financial	22%
5. Deep Water	22%
6. Sickness	19%
7. Death	19%

Survey conducted by the *Times* of London

In the above survey conducted by the *London Times* we see that people are more fearful of speaking in front of an audience than they are of dying. In other words, they would rather die than speak. The sad part about this is that many of them do die when they speak.

And then there are times when the best thing said is nothing:

The difference between a successful career and a mediocre one, sometimes consists of 4 or 5 things a day left unsaid.
Anon.

If you are interested in a more indepth study on communication I highly recommend the book, *"You've Got To Be Believed To Be Heard,"* written by Mr. Bert Decker. Mr. Decker's book was instrumental in the development of this chapter.

CHAPTER 19

Technology

If you are going to play the game to win in today's fast paced, ever changing world, then you are going to have to equip yourself with the proper tools. Fax machines, desktop and laptop computers, mobile phones, LCD projectors, modems, CD-ROMS, the Internet, Web Sites, multi-media presentations, scan machines, bar codes, banking by computer, video conferencing, digital imagery, color copies, and Virtual Reality technology are all common place today.

To learn how to equip yourself, go to school. Most major computer retail outlets have classes you can sign up for to learn how to use the hardware and software that you need to purchase. The amount of time you will devote learning how to use this new technology will be infinitesimal compared to what it will do for you. It will give you faster, quicker, better, more professional, increased productivity, increased profits, making more time available for you to dedicate to other things.

So, get out there and start taking advantage of the incredible technology that is available today. It will be frustrating at times, you may feel stupid at times, but it will be worth it.

Oh, and one minor point: **YOUR SUCCESS DEPENDS ON IT!**

(Refer also to Chapter 2 on Handling Change)

CHAPTER 20

If They Like You They Will Learn

Think back and remember you favorite teachers. Why were they your favorite? Was it because …

⇒   They made your life miserable
⇒   You hated going to their class
⇒   It was never any fun
⇒   They were always condescending toward you
⇒   They showed partiality
⇒   Laughter was forbidden

Those weren't the reasons that came to my mind. They may have been tough and demanding, but they were also fair, funny, interesting, challenging and smart.

◆   I looked forward to being in their class
◆   I liked being there
◆   I respected them
◆   I liked them
◆   I learned

If that's the way you remembered your favorite teachers why do you think teaching any other way would be more effective.

Create the WANT TO not the HAVE TO.

CHAPTER 21

Expectations ... Great Expectations

Zero defects, now that's Great Expectations, but it is what we should all be shooting for. Some of you may be saying that is ridiculous, zero defects is impossible. 80% right is darn good, 90% right is super, and 99.9% right is sensational. Let's take a look at 99.9% and just what that represents.

◆ 811,000 rolls of faulty 35mm film will be loaded this year.

◆ 1,314 phone calls will be misplaced every minute.

◆ 12 babies will be given to the wrong parents each day.

◆ 268,500 defective tires will be shipped this year.

◆ 14,208 defective personal computers will be shipped this year.

◆ Two unsafe plane landings daily at O'Hare International Airport.

◆ 18,322 pieces of mail will be misplaced in the next hour.

◆ 291 pacemaker operations will be performed incorrectly this year.

◆ 20,000 incorrect drug prescriptions will be written this year.

◆ 114,500 mismatched pairs of shoes will be shipped this year.

◆ $761,900 will be spent on tapes and compact discs that won't play.

◆ 107 incorrect medical procedures will be performed every day.

◆ 315 entries in Webster's *Third New International* edition will be misspelled.

So when you start to consider the real implications of just being .1% wrong, our objective for SEEKING EXCELLENCE, zero defects, 100% right, becomes essential. Expectations or Great Expectations ... the choice is yours.

Whatever you can do, or dream you can ... begin it.
Boldness has genius, power and magic in it.

Goethe

There is no more direct way of elevating our life
than by elevating our ideas.

Ernest Dimnet

Security is mostly a superstition.
It does not exist in nature,
nor do children of men as a whole experience it.
Avoiding danger is no safer in the long run
than outright exposure.
Life is either a daring adventure or nothing.

Helen Keller

The only limit to our realization of tomorrow
will be our doubts today.

Franklin D. Roosevelt

Don't measure yourself by what you have accomplished,
but by what you should have accomplished
with your ability.

John Wooden

Whether you think you can or think you can't,
you are right.

Henry Ford

**The credit belongs to the man
who is actually in the arena;
whose face is marred
by dust and sweat and blood;
who strives valiantly;
who errs and comes short again and again;
who knows the great enthusiasms,
the great devotions,
and spends himself in a worthy cause;
who at the best knows in the end
the triumph of high achievement;
and who at the worst, if he fails, at least fails
while daring greatly.**

Theodore Roosevelt

Expectations or Great Expectations ... again, it's your choice.

CHAPTER 22

Preparation

Georgia Tech invited 20 aerospace engineers and college professors to a paper airplane flying contest to see who could design a paper airplane to stay up the longest. A contest had also been conducted for second graders in the state of Georgia to see who could design a paper airplane and fly it the longest. The seven year old boy who won that contest was invited to Georgia Tech to compete with the aerospace engineers.

After they all made their paper airplanes and flew them to record their times ... 20 aerospace engineers and professors were embarrassed when the second grade boy, came in first place with his **Double Delta Flyer.** His paper airplane flew for 4.3 seconds and missed the longest time ever recorded in history by half a second. When the contingency of engineers and professors came over to question the small boy about how he did it, he said, *"I don't know."* So they went to his mother and asked how her 7 year old son beat 20 aerospace engineers and college professors. She said, *"Since he was 5 years old he has made over 2,000 paper airplanes ... so I guess he who makes the most planes wins."*

You want to be a gold medal winner in gymnastics; preparation that is required - about eight years of training, six hours per day. The same is true of all great athletes; years of training/preparation. Preparation required to become a concert pianist, approximately seventeen years. Great attorneys, doctors, lawyers, Realtors, artists, computers analysts, chefs, teachers, managers, bosses, etc., don't just happen; the more they prepare the better they will be. The same will be true for you.

Proper preparation is very simply the critical ingredient in the success formula. Now that's not to say that diligent preparation will insure that you are successful, but it is to say that *the lack of proper preparation* will almost certainly lead to failure.

Proper preparation also helps to reduce stress. So many people put everything off to the last minute and then try to pull off a miracle. The pressure mounts, little mistakes become giant problems because they have left themselves no time.

I don't think it is appropriate for companies to allow their people to learn at the expense of their customers, but companies do it every day. Many companies today have their employees face the customer long before they are prepared.

I can't tell you how many times I have been in a restaurant, department store, or car dealership and had some rookie try to assist me. Don't you find it annoying when you ask, *"What is the soup for the day?"* and they don't know. Car dealerships have a lot of salespeople just standing around waiting for you. These people are usually just passing the time waiting on the next person to drive up. Why aren't they studying? Why aren't they learning the answers to the most obvious questions? Why aren't they in the cars, studying the product they are supposed to be selling.

Salespeople should never be allowed to go learn how to sell at the expense of the customer. They should have studied extensively before ever being allowed to address the potential customer. If I can't get the answers I am looking for from the salesperson, then I will go some place I can.

Please understand I realize a rookie salesperson cannot know nor had time to develop all the skills a veteran salesperson has. But they can know their product/service inside and out. They may miss closing signals or may not be as confident as the veteran, but they should at least know their product/service.

A company is being graded by the consumer at every point of contact they have with that company. If I am dealing with a person who has not been properly trained to deal with me, how should I feel about the rest of the organization?

I remember walking up to the counter of a major hotel chain and having the front desk person ask me if I wouldn't mind having a trainee check me in. I told them that depends on how much training the trainee already had. They told me it was their first day. I said, *"Is this your first day on the job or your first day behind the counter after having been thoroughly trained in all aspects of checking a guest in along with a great deal of practice on the steps required to check me in using their computer?"* She said it was her first day on the job. I then told them that I did mind.

Why would I want to spend an extra 5, 10 or 15 minutes helping to train their employee when they basically had spent none. I had been on the road all day, making airline connections, trying to get cabs, dealing with traffic and the weather. I wanted to get to my room, check back in with my office, call my family, and relax. I felt it was very inappropriate that they had even asked; but at least they did ask. Some companies just stick that person behind the desk and let them stumble, bumble and fall at our expense.

If you took a look at who were the top Fortune 500 companies in 1970 to see where they are today, you would find that 60% of them are either gone or worse off. They may stumble, bumble and fall at our expense once …. But they will stumble, bumble and fall at their own expense in the long run.

To me it is simple:

Without proper preparation there can be no success.

Eagles Do This
Turkeys Don't

CHAPTER 23

Salesmanship

The Answers to Successful Selling Are All Four Letter Words.

Do they **WANT** something? Do they **NEED** something? Can we **HELP THEM FIND** out that they really **WANT** or **NEED** something? The art, discipline, and techniques of selling have traveled many different paths over the centuries. Thousands upon thousands of books have been written on the subject and thousands more will be written on it. Books dealing with the techniques of *High Pressure Selling, Manipulative Selling, Consultative Selling, Strategic Selling, SPIN Selling, Power Close Selling, and Emotional Selling* are ever present on the book store shelves and in libraries throughout the world.

I am finding through my studies and working with businesses that the path to selling effectively has gone from simple to highly sophisticated and back again. I don't mean to oversimplify the process of selling something, but I think that we can be more effective by sticking to the basics.

I'm sure you have all heard the golden rule, *"Do unto others as you would have them do unto you."* Unfortunately, due to greed, competition, and pressure to succeed, this axiom has changed in many cases to *"Do unto others to help yourself and then bug out,"* which is <u>insuring eventual failure</u>. Selling is both an ART and a SCIENCE but if you start out remembering the two basic principals of selling you will <u>insure your longevity</u> in this fine profession; they are ...

#1 - CARE   #2 - HELP

**I truly *care* about my customer and therefore
it is my responsibility to *help* them.**

Remember - the answers to successful selling are all Four Letter Words.

SHOW THEM ... DON'T TELL THEM

SEEK to FIND out their situation

LOOK to see how and if you can HELP

WORK HARD

GIVE MORE

LEAD THEM

MAKE CALL after CALL after CALL

GIVE MORE ... TAKE LESS

FEEL WHAT THEY FEEL ... HEAR WHAT THEY HEAR

LOVE what you are doing

Let THEM TALK

KNOW WHAT you SELL

JUST CARE MORE

I Am a Salesman

I am proud to be a salesman because more than any other person I, and millions of others like me, built America.

The person who builds a better mousetrap - or a better anything - would starve to death if they waited for people to beat a pathway to their door. Regardless of how good, or how needed, the product or service might be, it has to be sold.

Eli Whitney was laughed at when he showed the cotton gin. Edison had to install his electric light free of charge in an office building before anyone would look at it. The first sewing machine was smashed to pieces by a Boston mob. People scoffed at the idea of railroads. They thought that even traveling thirty miles an hour would stop the circulation of the blood! McCormick strived for fourteen years to get people to use his reaper. Westinghouse was considered a fool for stating that he could stop a train with wind. Morse had to plead before ten Congresses before they would even look at his telegraph.

The public didn't go around demanding these things; they had to be sold!

They needed thousands of salesmen, trailblazers, pioneers: people who could persuade with the same effectiveness as the inventor could invent. Salesmen took these inventions, sold the public on what these products could do, taught customers how to use them, and even taught businessmen how to make a profit from them.

As a salesman I've done more to make America what it is today than any other person you know. I was just as vital in your great-great-grandfather's day as I am in yours, and I'll be just as vital in your great-great-grandson's day. I have educated more people; created more jobs; taken more drudgery from the laborer's work; given more profits to businessmen; and given more people a fuller and richer life than anyone in history. I've dragged prices down, pushed quality up, made it possible for you to enjoy the comforts and luxuries of automobiles, radios, electric refrigerators, televisions, and air-conditioned homes and buildings. I've healed the sick, given security to the aged, and put thousands of young men and women through college. I've made it possible for inventors to invent, for factories to hum, and for ships to sail the seven seas.

How much money you find in your pay envelope next week, and whether in the future you will enjoy the luxuries of pre-fabricated homes, stratospheric flying airplanes, and a new world of jet propulsion and atomic power, depends on me. The loaf of bread that you bought today was on the baker's shelf because I made sure the farmer's wheat got to a mill, that the mill made the wheat into flour, and that the flour was delivered to your baker.

Without me the wheels of industry would come to a grinding halt. And with that, jobs, marriages, politics, and freedom of thought would be a thing of the past. I AM A SALESMAN and I'm both proud and grateful that as such I serve my family, my fellow man, and my country.

AUTHOR UNKNOWN

Hiring or Making
the
Eagle Salesperson

I've heard it time and time again that *"he was a natural born salesman"* or *"she's a natural at selling"* and nothing could be further from the truth. The more natural they look the harder they have worked at it. Probably what annoys me the most about the hiring practices of corporate America is that they are looking for that **natural born salesperson** because they want to spend as little time as possible in training them. The old three days of training and a pat on the back is still a prominent habit in preparing salespeople for the marketplace today. Then, to top that off, if they really don't have the time to spend to train them properly, the sales manager puts them in the field with a so called <u>seasoned veteran</u> who is guaranteed to make them a success; just watch and do what they do.

When it is all said and done, they are putting someone in the field who is going to have to learn their trade at the expense of the customer; and they wonder why their sales are low. How would they like to go to a doctor and have him learn surgery at the expense of their life? If the doctor has only three days of training the likelihood of their dying on the operating table is extremely high. The same is true in the sales arena. The likelihood of that new salesperson killing off existing clients or potential ones is extremely high.

What should they really be looking for in a salesperson? The following is my short list. Later on in this chapter I will give you my long list.

▲ They want it...Success / Money / Prestige.

▲ Smarts...the ability to learn about **your** product or service.

▲ Ability to follow instruction.

▲ Accepting of constructive criticism.

▲ Can accept changes in both business and personal matters.

▲ Listens extremely well.

▲ Not assuming.

▲ Always looking for a better way.

▲ Able to take responsibility for their mistakes.

▲ A student of people, business, your products/services and constantly strives to add to their knowledge.

▲ Stingy with their time.

▲ Able to manage their territory rather than their territory managing them.

▲ A team player.

▲ Honest with themselves, their customers and their company.

▲ Understanding the importance of follow-up.

▲ Aware that selling is an acquired skill that must be constantly practiced, studied and critiqued to realize improvement.

I am certain there is not a person reading this book that couldn't come up with other characteristics they would like to see in a salesperson. But if you analyze the list you should notice that there are only a few items that can't be learned or should I say ***taught***.

You can't teach *WANT, IQ, or HONESTY* but the rest is teachable. The first thing you have to ask yourself is how much money can you afford to spend in properly training your sales force. Then you need to consider how much time will be required to make them what they need to be in order to *not kill the customer*.

The second question has a lot to do with the caliber and experience level of the person you hire, but remember high caliber and experience usually come at a high price. So let's proceed on the premise that we can't afford to hire the superstar; you've got to make them.

The first mistake that is usually made is that you hire and start training before you are ready. You expect your salesperson to be organized so you need to set the example and have a structured, well planned out training program set up before you bring them on board. You need to walk yourself through several sales calls and address what it is they are really going to be doing. You need to write up or have available, their: *(will vary by industry - but worth reviewing)*

- Job description
- Company mission statement
- Company brochures / price lists
- Sales manual with policies and procedures to follow
- A sale's call script ... structure of a sale's call, etc.
- Top 10 objections and script on how to overcome them
- How you expect them to service accounts and acquire new accounts
- Have testimonial letters from satisfied customers copied for them...if available
- A phone script for cold calling potential new customers
- A complete explanation on how they get paid, commissions, etc.
- A complete explanation on how to submit expenses and when they will be reimbursed
- How you expect them to handle call reports

Let me give you an example of how the simplest thing can get overlooked because top management thinks, *that's so simple, they know that,* but they really don't. I usually start out all my training sessions with one question that everyone in the room should know and the answer should be similar when stated by each person. But it never is. If the group is large enough I try and get five people aside in a separate room before the main session begins and then pull one at a time, of the five, out of that room into another room totally isolating them from everyone. This room has a video camera in it which is ready to film them. I then read to each of the five participants, when they are in the room with me alone, the following statement:

"You are at your prospective client's office ... and they say ...

'I have spoken to your two main competitors and they have told me why I should do business with them. Tell me why I should do business with you? How long have you been in business? Exactly what is it that your company does?'"

They have no more than 2 minutes to reply and remember, their response is being videotaped. I then ask them to go get another salesperson and have them come in. I make it very clear that they are not to discuss anything that has just happened. I explain to them that by telling their associates what just took place would help them be better prepared for the exercise and possibly make their associates response better than theirs.

You would be absolutely amazed at the magnitude of difference in the responses we record. All of them work for the same company, but yet by their responses it would be hard to prove that. After I get everyone's answer on tape I then bring them all back in the room and show the tape of all responses. Some are proud of what they said, some are disappointed, some are ashamed, but they all learn from the exercise.

Then we go over the tape again and instruct them to take notes on what they feel are the strong, useful, and great statements made by each other. Now it's time to write up the **School Solution** of what **"they all"** should be saying. The key factor is that **"they"** are writing it up, with some assistance from the trainer, therefore **"they"** are more likely to use it because **"they"** helped create it.

When I show the first video tape to the owners, VP of Marketing or Sales, they can't believe what they are hearing. Forget how the message was delivered, they are totally shocked at the content of the message. Something so obvious as to what the company does is being handled incorrectly.

Never assume that because you know it they will, or because they've said it or heard it, they will remember it. It takes a great deal of practice to develop a top notch sales force, but it is well worth it. Strive to make your sales force govern each other. Tell them that they need to be proud of each other. Explain to them that a weak link will hurt them all, so they need to help each other and learn from each other.

Have them do infield sales audits of each other and write up what they are seeing. The object here is to identify as many strengths as they can find and then identify the two most important things the person audited needs to work on. If you give someone a list of 5, 8 10 things they are doing wrong you kill the most important strength of a salesperson; confidence.

If you feel you are not capable of putting together these materials and/or training your people, then hire an outside consultant who can. Many entrepreneurs today are finding that they do not need a full-time VP of Sales to have an effective sales force. They are hiring from the outside for a fraction of the cost and getting better results.

Regardless of how you intend to hire, remember to give them a stimulating, positive environment to work in with constant reinforcement. I have never found fear to be a long term motivator. People have got to want to do it, to make it happen. The *Eagle* salesperson strives to be what Carl Jung called a "conscious competent." This is someone who is good at what he or she does, but is constantly trying to improve.

Professional athletes who dominate their sports during and after their prime understand this concept. They work out a little harder, take a hundred extra swings during practice or are on the putting green hours after the lesser competitors have gone home.

It doesn't matter if you are going to hire or make the *Eagle* salesperson for your company, you still have to be prepared for them.

What is the Eagle Salesperson ?

They are not born, **they are made.**

Understand persistence alone will not insure their success.

Likable, friendly, non-threatening.

Constantly striving to improve.

Recognize the importance of the open mind.

They **aren't narrow-minded,** assuming they have all the answers.

Continue their education.

Receptive and **unafraid** to try new things or entertain new ideas.

Always looking for a better way to do just about everything, but especially for a better way to serve their clients.

Set goals recognizing the power of expressing their goals in writing, being careful to make them challenging, but achievable.

Dreamers; but their dreams are real-world, appreciating the steps necessary to make them happen.

Analyze their own performance. After a call they will spend a few moments reflecting on what went wrong and what went right, and then make the necessary adjustments for the next call.

Make brief notes about their meeting with the client to **keep up a current profile** and will consult with that profile before speaking to them again.

Don't beat themselves up when things go wrong.

Take responsibility for mistakes instead of blaming everyone around them.

Learn from their mistakes and keep their self-esteem high by working to avoid reoccurrence.

Student of people. They understand the importance of developing rapport with a client; that a client is looking for trust, confidence and understanding. They realize that when we see things the same way as someone else, we fall into a neurological sameness which in turn makes us seem very likable to another. They know that by being on the same wavelength as someone else, they have an excellent probability of being able to influence that person.

Have a good understanding of the primary representational systems people use to decipher information; Visual, Auditory and Kinesthetic and look for accessing cues so they can disseminate information in the primary system.

Student of business. This just doesn't mean knowing your product, but also your competitors products or services they offer, the economy's impact on sales, pending legislation that could effect the sale, and financing. They understand that **the use of knowledge is power in selling**, and that clients will be attracted to the most knowledgeable salespeople because they can always get their questions answered.

Meet needs, they just don't push for the sale.

Ask questions before offering suggestions, realizing that it is critical to uncover the client's Situation, seeing if there are any Problems with that Situation, having the client identify the Implications of those Problems and then having the client state they have a Need. Throughout this entire process they skillfully utilize the art of listening.

Excellent listener. They guide a conversation by asking appropriate questions. They clarify their understanding of what the client said to make sure they heard properly and, above all, they don't talk when they should be listening. There is no more valuable a tool in selling than listening. The good salesperson **contains their desire to talk**, knowing that listening is the purpose of the call. They wait for the appropriate moment to deliver their solutions based on the needs they discovered.

They eliminate objections before they arise by asking probing questions that build value in the product or service they are offering. They realize that objections about value are due to not developing the needs of the client strongly enough. They understand that the majority of objections are only a symptom caused by poor selling skills. They are also aware that objection-handling skills will always have a part to play in a sales call, therefore, they have identified and memorized the answers to the most common objections they receive and learned how to present those answers in a manner not offending to the client.

Sell Wisdom, Knowledge, Service, Integrity, Understanding and Concern rather than Product, Price, Sizzle and Hype.

Many people believe that price is the only thing the client is after. Price is obviously important, but it will seldom overcome the trust, confidence and concern that a real salesperson demonstrates in the handling of the entire selling process. Sure there are companies that sell entirely on price and they will do a lot of business, but they won't really need *great* salespeople. The true professional will also **uncover the concerns other than price** that do exist and make sure they, too, are also taken care of. By taking care of all the concerns in the beginning, they know they are **developing a long term client** who will also **refer them business**.

Selfish with their time realizing that this precious resource is irreplaceable, and therefore, must be used wisely.

Excellent at **follow-up**. They do what they say they will do, when they say they will do it.

Understand the power of personal touch and find out what is important in the lives of their clients and play to that importance. The simple task of sending birthday cards, thanks for the business cards, special occasion cards, and thinking of you cards are of monumental importance to the *Eagle* salesperson; they never fail to keep in touch.

Understand and appreciate the differences between features and benefits. Features are the specific components of a product or service that may result in benefits for the user. Typical salespeople state the features without mentioning the benefits to the client, leaving it up to the client to understand them; it is not the customer's responsibility to know these things, it is the salesperson's job to explain them. They **never forget that** *"people do business for their reasons, not ours."* They sell benefits, not merely features.

Team players seeing themselves as part of a well-maintained machine.

Generous with praise among the other team members, and they support the team when they are in the field.

Don't blame problems on other people; they pitch in and take action whenever possible to resolve conflicts and problems.

Show respect for the people they work with by expressing appreciation for jobs well done.

Avoid talking down the competition because it is unprofessional and reflects more on the accuser than the accused.

Honest with their company, their client and themselves, striking a balance in their relationships between clients and their company. They know that they need their client to sell to and their company to have something to sell. They must represent both fairly to succeed over the long haul.

Work hard and play hard, for they are aware of the benefits of a well-balanced life. They understand that maintaining a proper balance of personal and professional priorities is a sure way to avoid burnout and keep them motivated; smelling the roses is just as important as working hard.

When it comes to being a skilled, professional, Eagle Salesperson ... how do you compare?

CHAPTER 24

You Get What You Pay For

I flew on an airline today on which I have never flown. I've heard a lot about the airline and why it is so successful. Their president is a wild and crazy guy who loves to have fun and wants his employees to do the same. He has proven you can make money in the airline industry and I must say I have been impressed with everything I have ever read about this man and his company.

Well today I got to experience the company first hand. I didn't know it, but you can't get a boarding pass ahead of time. You have to wait in line to get one. I waited 29 minutes. I would have paid more to have had a boarding pass pre-issued.

There is no such thing as first class with this airline. All the seats are the same; small. I would have paid more for a first class seat.

My *"issued at the gate"* boarding pass was number 61, which I came to find out later, meant that I was in the last group to board. 1-30 go first. 30-60 next and then the people above 60. I would have paid more to have been able to get on board early to insure that I had overhead space for my two bags.

I would have paid more to sit up front and not have to wait for almost the entire plane to unload before I got off.

The plane was late due to poor weather in the place it was leaving from; so what else is new.

Today something was played out right before my very eyes that explains why we have so many economic choices in our economy. This airline company was filling a demand for airline service designed to get people from point A to point B as inexpensively as possible. This airline company realizes that there are lots of people who are willing to put up with a lot of inconveniences to get from point A to point B as inexpensively as possible. This airline was doing an excellent job fulfilling that need.

I just wanted to leave at a specific time and this airline was leaving then. Next time I will give more consideration to what I will be giving up in order to travel at the time I want to travel. I have other needs that this airline doesn't fulfill, needs I've already explained. You get what you pay for folks most of the time. In this particular case, I would have paid more to have gotten more ... but that was not their agenda.

Airlines

Since we're on the subject of airlines let's delve a little further. I guess you could define their function as: *getting you from point A to point B via the air, safely, comfortably, leaving at a certain time, arriving at a certain time.* Safely and comfortably are subject to definition, but timeliness can definitely be measured. All in all I feel that the airlines do a pretty good job. There are many variables they have to deal with, that many times, are not under their control; the biggest being weather. These many variables effect the job they do and the way we feel about the job they do.

You shouldn't blame the airlines for the idiot you had to sit beside on your last trip; but some of us do. And for the food, what do you expect from a kitchen the size of a broom closet. You shouldn't blame them about the weather; they have nothing to do with it. The bumpy ride due to air-turbulence is not their fault. And you should lighten up on the flight attendants when they aren't in the best of moods; they have to deal with an abundance of difficult people. What do I like most about airline travel? Well, let's see. I like ...

- ◈ Frequent flyer programs
- ◈ Not having to drive
- ◈ Getting places fast
- ◈ The *first class* section

In describing what I like least about them, I must note that these are not company specific complaints, but rather experiences I have either witnessed or endured over my many years of air travel. With that said, here goes:

First and foremost is their policy to not let you in on what is really happening. If the plane is going to be leaving late, they never will tell you exactly how late. They always string you along. This is a practice that is industry wide.

Delays due to mechanical failures
Dirty smelly rest rooms
Lost luggage
Destroyed luggage
Limited overhead luggage space

The luggage carried on by the flight attendants. I understand they have to bring their bags on the plane. I understand they have to have a place to store them. I do not understand when the place they store them is right above my seat. And let me give you fair warning, NEVER EVER SUGGEST for them to move their bag from above your seat so you can put your bag there. If you value your life, don't do it.

Overbooking is a standard practice today. You need to be aware that having a ticket with no accompanying boarding pass does not guarantee you a seat on the plane. I watched a plane fly off without two ticketed *Platinum Frequent Flyers* being on board that plane; I was one of them. A teenager who showed up at the gate 20 minutes after we did and got on that plane because he had a boarding pass and we didn't. He might fly the airline two or three times that year, we would be on it over a hundred times. Let's just say we weren't real happy.

I shouldn't complain though. Yes, they are sometimes late. Yes, they are sometimes rude. Yes, the food is sometimes inferior.

But, YES, they get me where I want to go, very fast, in an approximate frame of time, over 90% of the time ... and that is the most important aspect of what I am paying for.

My rules for dealing with the airlines are simple.

- [ ] Be the first on the plane if at all possible.
- [ ] Carry only two bags that WILL fit in the overhead.
- [ ] Order their lowfat meal in advance.
- [ ] Have a light jacket in easy access for cold planes.
- [ ] Carry a laptop computer and/or reading materials to work on.
- [ ] Wear dark clothes to hide drink and food spills.
- [ ] **Bring a few smiles and share them.**

Chapter 25

8 / 16 Rule

I heard it once said,

> *"If you do a good job people will go tell 8 people,*
> *but if you do a bad job*
> *they'll go warn 16."*

I have no idea if these figures can be substantiated, but I do know that doing a good job is your best, cheapest and most effective form of advertising.

Who better to do business with than people who:

- ▣ Do more than expected.
- ▣ Always seem to go above and beyond what is necessary.
- ▣ Were genuinely concerned about us.
- ▣ Follow up after, to make sure everything is "still" fine.
- ▣ Return our calls promptly regardless of circumstances.

Your greatest form of advertising is the job you do everyday.

Actions speak louder than words.

Service speaks louder than advertising.

Caring gets me telling others about you
and not caring
gets me warning others about you.

The day we forget

we are in business

because of the

customer

is the day

we start

going out

of business.

Robert Stevenson

Section III

Fine Tuning

Your Game

CHAPTER 26

Enthusiasm

Emerson said, *"Nothing great is ever achieved without enthusiasm."* I see enthusiasm as the critical trait, component, ingredient in the personality of successful people. Enthusiasm is the gas that drives your engine on your journey towards SEEKING EXCELLENCE. With enthusiasm, you will forever have the chance to succeed, without it you have failed before you ever started.

Some people show it differently than others, but that doesn't mean it is any less powerful or they are any less committed. Webster's defines it this way:

enthusiasm: 1. originally, supernatural inspiration or possession. 2. intense or eager interest; zeal; fervor. — *SYN.* see passion.

zeal: ardent endeavor or devotion. — *SYN.* see passion.

fervor: 1. intense heat. 2. great warmth of emotion; ardor; zeal.— *SYN.* see passion.

emotion: 1. Strong, generalized feeling; physical excitement.— *SYN.* see feeling

ardor: 1. Emotional warmth; passion; eagerness; enthusiasm; zeal. — *SYN.* see passion.

passion: 5. Extreme, compelling, emotion; intense emotional drive or excitement. — *SYN.* fervor, ardor, enthusiasm, zeal.

In looking at how Webster's defines enthusiasm and the words associated to the term, it is obvious to see a pattern developing towards another word, PASSION; they go hand-in-hand. You can't have one without the other. And so it is with Success — you can't have success without enthusiasm; they go hand-in-hand.

Enthusiasm is but a state of mind, the combination between mental and physical energy; your belief (the mental) put into action (physical energy).

Enthusiasm is the yeast that makes
your hope rise to the stars.

Enthusiasm is the sparkle in your eyes,
it is the swing in your gait,
the grip of your hand,
the irresistible surge of your will and
your energy to execute your ideas.

Enthusiasts are fighters.
They have fortitude.
They have staying qualities.

Enthusiasm is at the bottom
of all progress!

With it there is accomplishment.
Without it there are only alibis...

Henry Ford's Fireplace Motto

CHAPTER 27

You Gotta Learn To Laugh

One of the biggest problems in America today is that we don't laugh enough. I heard it said once *that a child laughs 300 times a day while an adult laughs only 30.* Now I can't say for a fact that this is true by way of a clinical study, but I can tell you by personal observation that children laugh a lot more than adults.

Some personal observations I can speak of were when my son Tyler was a child; not only Tyler, but his friends as well. When he was playing, he was laughing. When he was playing with his friends, they were laughing. The movies he watched were mostly designed to make him laugh as well as the cartoons and other television children's shows. He wanted to play, have fun, and laugh a lot.

Somewhere between our infancy to adulthood we supposedly mature and start approaching life in a more serious manner, therefore, greatly diminishing the occurrence of this wonderfully healthy emotion. We don't quit laughing because we want to. We have this emotion almost surgically removed from us by our parents, grandparents, school teachers, administrators, bosses and the like. They kept telling us to *"be quiet,"* or to *"take this serious,"* or *"you can't be having that much fun and getting anything accomplished."* The list goes on and on.

Whoever came up with the notion that for businesses to be successful they have to be serious, boring enterprises providing jobs of drudgery, needs to go back to the caveman era. Small companies, organizations, associations and large corporations are finding out that laughter in the workplace is good. Elevating your organization to a place that's fun to come to, has proven to be not only a productive strategy but a profitable one as well. It has also proven to be a very healthy strategy for the organization as well as the individual. (remember Chapter 5)

Our educational system needs to add a chapter in its training manual on incorporating humor into the learning process. I feel that you will learn more in a class you enjoy going to compared to a class where the teacher just drives the information down your throat.

So lighten-up and laugh more. People like doing business with people who are happy folks. Just remember this one rule ... laughter at the expense of another person is not acceptable.

Eagles Do This
Turkeys Don't

CHAPTER 28

Having A Bad Day
Why Me ... Life Is Terrible

So you're having a bad day; I can assure you there is someone else out there that is having a worse day. This fact may or may not make you feel better, but it's true. I guess the big question is how should we handle a bad day?

I would first try and identify the cause of the bad day. What has triggered your emotional response? Has someone said something or done something to you? Just exactly what has caused you to feel the way you are feeling? I would then recommend that you re-evaluate your current emotional state. Ask yourself; five years from now will this really matter? In your past, have you lived through something similar to this situation? If so, how did you handle it and how did it turn out?

I'm not here to tell you that you should never have a bad day; hey, they are going to happen. The objective here is to keep them few and far between. But I do have one real big suggestion that is certain to change your state of mind if you can't seem to get out of the BAD DAY feeling. Go visit a children's cancer ward at any hospital and talk to some of the nurses about the status of several of their patients. You want a reality check fast, this is a sure cure.

Time and time again, we hear of stories about how unfair life is. I realize we're all going to have some bad days; without a couple of bad days thrown in once in a while, how would we appreciate the good days?

When thinking about bad days, try and concentrate on how lucky you are to have any days at all. The alternative isn't too favorable. There is a list of people published everyday in the newspaper that would be happy to change places with you; it's called the Obituary.

THE COMPLAINER

This is wrong and that is wrong.
Oh, how they love to talk about what is wrong.

For you COMPLAINERS out there, let me share this thought with you. **20 percent of the people you tell don't care, and the other 80 percent are glad you're there.** Okay, maybe I'm being a little harsh. Maybe there is somebody out there who cares, but your complaining all the time isn't making their life any easier. So after a while, if you keep on complaining, they are going to quit caring, too.

There are some people out there that don't even realize they are complaining. To them, it is just *casual conversation* about the days' events. i.e.: Spouse comes home from work and interwoven in their opening salvo of HELLO are the following facts.

▶ *"Boy was traffic terrible ... I hate driving to work."*
▶ *"This stupid jerk cut me off and I spilled my coffee."*
▶ *"I was late for the 9:00 meeting ... my boss was upset."*
▶ *"That one jerk put me behind schedule all day."*
▶ *"My suit wasn't ready at the cleaners that I need tomorrow."*

The list can go on and on.

My question to you complainers out there is ... *What do you expect the person you're telling this to, to say or do?*

- ▣ *"I'm so sorry you had a bad day."*
- ▣ *"Oh, I hate to hear that."*
- ▣ *"What a shame ... you must feel awful."*
- ▣ *"Is there anything I can do to help?"*

Usually when we ask if there is anything we can do to help, the complainer says, *"NO."* If the answer is no, then why are they telling us? And, the other three answers, now those really help a lot.

I realize that sometimes you really need to "VENT" your frustrations about the day's events to feel better, blow off a little steam, but to do it everyday, day in and day out, is not being fair to the person to whom you are "VENTING ON."

I have a friend whose wife use to complain all the time. She was a classic *Casual Conversational Complainer.* She always put the days events in a negative tone, which made it difficult to have an enjoyable evening together. He tried telling her she was complaining too much, but she always said she didn't. *"What are you talking about ... I very seldom complain,"* would be her rebuttal. The fact was, she really didn't realize just how negative she was. So he decided to show her how often she complained.

He bought a very sensitive, small hand held tape recorder that could be hidden easily, but would still record clearly, anything she said. When she came home he had it out of sight and on, so he could record her *supposedly never complaining dialogue.* He did it three nights in a row, to prove beyond a shadow of any doubt, that she had become a *habitual casual conversational complainer.*

He thought he was going to have to edit the tapes so they wouldn't have to listen to all the non-complaining conversation during playback, but that wasn't necessary. The first five minutes of each of the three tapes provided plenty of examples of her complaining.

I couldn't believe he had the guts to play the tapes back. He said that in order to soften the situation, before playing the tapes back, he told her that he loved her dearly and just wanted to show her something about herself that he knew she didn't realize. He said that they even laughed about it afterwards. It must have worked because they are still together seventeen years later. *(I am not recommending this at all ... just sharing the incident)*

We all are going to complain at one time or another. Sometimes it is good to complain, to get it off your chest. But that complaining is usually only good for you. The receiver of the negative dialogue is having no fun listening. So, before you open your mouth and respond when someone asks, *"how are you doing"* or *"how was your day,"* think about how your next words are going to effect the both of you. If they are negative words, you are going to possibly relive the experience and feel even worse than you currently do, and also help to *bring down* the person you are sharing them with.

So when people ask ... *"How are you doing,"* try responding this way.

- *"Great, but getting better."*
- *"Just happy to be here."*
- *"Looking forward to now."*
- *"Super."*
- *"Fantastic."*
- *"Wonderful ... thanks for asking."*

Don't forget, when you think you are having a bad day, there is a whole list of people in the paper ready to trade places with you.

One final suggestion. If you still can't get out of your depressive, negative ways, try taking a few minutes and writing down everything you have going for you. When I do this, everything takes on a better perspective.   i.e.:

◈ I'm breathing (*key point*)
◈ My health is good.
◈ I can walk, talk, see and hear.

My list goes on and on and on. I have so much to be thankful for; shame on me for ever complaining.

Shame on you, too.

Remember, people don't like to be around complainers.

Complaining,
it's your choice.

CHAPTER 29

Gift Giving

This one really gets to me. It seems to many people out there that the *Rule of Thumb* for giving a gift is *"How much did they spend on us last year?"* What has that got to do with the price of milk in Russia?

Giving should have nothing to do with getting. If giving has something to do with getting, then it isn't really giving.

I talked already about mentors ... well I have a mentor in my life on giving: my wife Annie. She never ceases to amaze me. She is always thinking about other people and what she can do to help out, brighten a day, or just simply remember them and let them know they are special. This is not to say she is extravagant or frivolous with our money; in fact that is quite the contrary. But when she can, she is ready to jump right in. What I like about her giving is the fact that she never mentions anything about what they have done for her or what she expects in return. A thank you would be nice, but if you forget, that's okay, because she was giving to give ... not to get. Her joy came in the picking out of the gift, wrapping it and shipping it to them. Her joy came in the anticipation of the happiness the gift would bring. And I know for a fact that if a family member or friend was in need she would be the first to help even if it meant her doing without.

I feel that gift giving is very important in business. It is not the expense of the gift that is important, but the fact that you went to the trouble to remember them. I also feel it is important to try and remember your client when everyone else isn't. During the holidays everyone tries to remember everyone else, so you won't really stand out. I'm not saying to forget that special time of the year, but I am suggesting you think of other times during the year that you remember your clients.

You might want to remember them on the anniversary date of their first order with you. If someone refers some business your way, send them a small token of your appreciation. If they are a close friend and they aren't expecting anything, send them something anyway.

If you are a manager that gets paid an override on the production, revenues or commissions your people generate, take a small portion of that money and return it back to your people in the form of a gift; I would recommend ten percent of the net override you received. That small reinvestment in them will reap you huge rewards.

CHAPTER 30

Achievement - Failure

It's Tough To Have One Without The Other

Beethoven's teacher called him a hopeless composer.

Albert Einstein's teacher described him as *"mentally slow, unsociable and adrift in foolish dreams."*

Henry Ford failed and went broke five times before he finally succeeded.

R.H. Macy failed seven times before his store in New York caught on.

Babe Ruth struck out 1,330 times, but also hit 714 home runs.

The testing director for MGM in 1933 wrote the following memo about Fred Astaire's first screen test: *"Can't act! Slightly bald! Can dance a little."* Mr. Astaire kept the memo over the fireplace in his home.

Walt Disney was fired by a newspaper editor for lack of ideas.

An expert once said of Vince Lombardi: *"He possesses minimal football knowledge and lacks motivation."*

Winston Churchill failed in sixth grade. He did not become Prime Minister of England until he was 62, and then only after a lifetime of defeats and setbacks. His greatest contributions came when he was a *senior citizen.*

In 1926, Lee de Forest, the man who invented the cathode ray tube, said, *"While theoretically television may be feasible, commercially and financially I consider it an impossibility, a development of which we need waste little time dreaming."*

In 1943, Thomas J. Watson, chairman of the board of IBM, said, *"I think there is a world market for about five computers."*

In 1945, Admiral William Leahy told President Truman about the atomic bomb: *"This is the biggest fool thing we've ever done - the bomb will never go off - and I speak as an expert on explosives."*

A recording company that turned down the Beatles in 1962 stated: *"We don't think they will do anything in their market. Guitar groups are on their way out."*

Marconi, the inventor of the radio, was considered insane and put in an insane asylum because of his idea that sounds of voices and music could be sent through the air. His theory could not be accepted by the vast majority. Although he was put in an insane asylum, it did not prove his idea was unworkable or laws of radio were not valid and did not exist, it just hindered progress. His idea was judged insane by others because it did not conform to what they believed or expected to be possible or true.

In the mid 1800's the head of the Patent Office in Washington recommended the Patent Office should be closed, because everything that could have been invented had already been invented ... and speaking of the Patent Office ...

When the Wright Brothers applied for a patent for their flying machine, it was rejected by the Patent Office. The Patent Office inspectors rejected it because they believed machines that were heavier than air could not fly.

It's been said that the power of an idea can be measured by the resistance it receives.

Average, middle-of-the-road, conservative people occupy this earth; the risk takers run it. **When you think it can't be done, think again.**

Success is not how high and fast

you reach the top,

but how high and fast

you bounce back

when you hit bottom.

Anon.

Did	is a word of achievement,
Won't	is a word of retreat,
Should've	is a word of bereavement,
Can't	is a word of defeat,
Ought	is a word of duty,
Try	is a word of each hour,
Will	is a word of beauty,
Can	is a word of power.

Anon.

Tom Watson, Sr., the founder of IBM, was being interviewed by a young man who asked the following question. *"Mr. Watson, how can I be great like you?"* Without any hesitation Mr. Watson responded, *"Double your failures."*

The greatest salespeople in any organization are the ones who have, in almost all cases, failed the most. The attitude of every *"NO"* takes you closer to the next *"YES"* is to me, the only way to look at life. Every supposed failure should be considered a learning experience. Now, I'm not talking about making the same mistake over and over again; I call that stupidity. But when you do fail, take some time and look at what has occurred. What can you learn from this experience? What did you do right? What did you do wrong? I have a friend in the real estate industry who I respect a great deal, Mrs. Ginger McQuigg. She rose up through the ranks until she became Vice President of one of the largest real estate companies in America with over 500 Realtors directly under her charge. Ginger is a CLASS act, and capitalizing the word CLASS still doesn't do her justice. One time we were discussing her career and I asked her how she became so successful. She told me that when she lost a sale, she called the prospect and asked why. Not to try and save the sale, but to truthfully learn something. She said sometimes they would tell her, sometimes they wouldn't, and sometimes she knew they were just feeding her lip-service. Ginger told me, the calls in which they explained why, were invaluable to her success.

There was a study in the Harvard Business Review in 1990 that stated: *"1 out of 26 customers complain, the other 25 just go somewhere else."* You need to know why they are going somewhere else. In fact, just by asking you may get a second shot at getting them back. Some people are amazingly forgiving when they know you care.

When I am up on stage delivering one of my programs, one of the greatest tools I can use to evaluate my program is that of a video camera. The camera doesn't lie. Sure I want to see what is having the greatest impact on the audience and what I am doing right. But more importantly, I want to see what I am doing wrong. Many times I am experimenting with new material and I want to see how it is being received. If it doesn't go over well, I may alter, tweak or eventually drop the material, but I never see it as a failure. I learn from it and move on.

<u>Portrait of an Achiever</u>

Failed in business - bankruptcy, 1831
Defeated for legislature, 1832
Failed in business - bankruptcy, 1833
Sweetheart - fiancee dies, 1835
Nervous breakdown, 1836
Defeated in election, 1838
Defeated for U.S. Congress, 1843
Defeated for U.S. Congress, 1846
Defeated again for U.S. Congress, 1848
Defeated for U.S. Senate, 1854
Defeated for U.S. Vice President, 1856
Defeated for U.S. Senate, 1858
Elected President of the U.S., 1860

Abraham Lincoln

While researching for his book *Think and Grow Rich*, the great writer Napoleon Hill discovered, that in most cases for over 500 millionaires he interviewed, success came after their greatest failure.

Learn from your mistakes. See them as stepping stones to your future successes. If you don't think it's really works, then go back to the beginning of the chapter and read it again. This isn't fiction folks, it's fact. At least it's fact to the EAGLES out there.

Eagles Do This
Turkeys Don't

CHAPTER 31

Your Personal Mission Statement

Now this might be a little heavy for you, but if you want to live a life that really matters, then you may want to give some thought to what your mission is. What would you like to accomplish during your short stay on this planet. In the overall scheme of things, in comparison to the amount of time our planet has been around and will be around, our time on this planet doesn't even represent as much as a blink of the eye. But yet, there are those who have made a difference for you and me. People who have come along and made our stay on this earth better in some shape, manner or form.

You've read about them in our history books. People reference their accomplishments in speeches. People strive to teach, train, and educate others about them. George Washington, Sandra Day O'Connor, Thomas Edison, Helen Keller, Martin Luther King, Amelia Earhart, Alexander Graham Bell, Margaret Thatcher, Tom Watson, Sr., Florence Nightingale, all have made a difference. They all had something in mind ... they all had a Personal Mission.

Sit down and decide what you stand for, where you want to go and why you want to go there. Sure I want to be a great husband and a super dad, but I also want more. I want to be remembered as a man who helped others reach their peak potential; especially helping those who felt they couldn't by showing them they could. I want to be remembered as a man who helped make this world a better place. *What do you want to be remembered for ... what are they going to say at your funeral?*

CHAPTER 32

The Power Of Praise And Recognition
Recognizing someone else's contribution will repay you doubly.

Adding *"Feelings"* Above The Line
Will Add *"Profits"* Below The Line

Have you ever been around someone who makes you feel good? A person that would make you say, *"I feel good about me, when I'm around you."* In our day to day quest for striving to beat the competition, to come up with an innovative idea, better service, faster response times, excellent value - sometimes we forget to take care of something that can have an even greater effect on our customers ... *our people*.

Ladies and gentlemen, it is a proven fact that people perform better when they feel better about themselves. When was the last time you gave out a compliment? Don't sit there and think that since your people are paid handsomely that compliments aren't necessary. Don't make excuses for not giving them out because you just don't have the time.

Let me put it in simple dollars and cents. Employees will treat customers exactly like management treats them. So treating employees special, making them feel good about themselves, has a direct reflection on the bottom line of any company.

If you want to Pump Up Your Profits then Pump Up Your People.

The number one reason people leave companies is not because of money; it's because of lack of recognition. Simple words like, *"Way to go," "You did a super job," "We couldn't have done it without you," "You sure are an asset to this company," "The contribution you made to this project has been invaluable,"* are far more effective than just paying them a little more. Just the simple word of THANKS goes a whole lot further than you can ever imagine.

If you are of the mind set that you don't want or need to be a cheerleader … that's their job … I pay them well so they better perform … then you better get use to training new people because you are going to be losing employees at a substantially higher percentage rate than the person/company that believes in recognizing and praising their employees.

You also need to remember the rule: ***Praise in public, criticize in private***. When you do have to criticize, don't just dwell on the negative; make sure you leave them with some compliments, too. Whenever I worked with people, I never tried to identify to them all the things they were doing wrong. I've always had the opinion that you can't fix everything at once, so why tell them all the things they are doing wrong at one time; possibly breaking their spirit. I felt my job was to identify in my mind everything that they were doing wrong, prioritize those things, and then tell them two things they should work on. Once those two things were fixed, I would move on to the next couple listed on my priority list.

I also feel it is critical to leave them in a positive frame of mind, mentioning things that they are really doing well. We all function better in a positive environment, feeling good about ourselves.

Dr. Benjamin Bloom of the University of Chicago studied 100 extraordinary young athletes, musicians, and students. He was surprised to find out that the young prodigies didn't begin by showing flashes of brilliance. Instead they received careful guidance, attention, and support and then they began to develop. The belief that they could be special came before any overt signs of any great talent.

The Best Memory System

Forget each kindness that you do as soon as you have done it:

Forget the praise that falls on you the moment you have won it.

Forget the slander that you hear before you repeat it:

Forget each slight, each spite, each sneer, wherever you may meet it.

Remember every kindness done to you, whatever its measure:

Remember praise by others won and pass it on with pleasure:

Remember every promise made and keep it to the letter:

Remember those who lend you aid and be a grateful debtor:

Remember all the happiness that comes your way in living:

Forget each worry and distress, be hopeful and forgiving:

Remember good,

Remember truth,

Remember heaven is above you,

And you will find, through age and youth, that many hearts will love you.

Anon.

Treat a man as he is and he will remain as he is. Treat a man as he can and should be and he will become as he can and should be.

Goethe

The reverse side of recognition and praise is blame. Regardless of your position, be it in management, associate, parent, teacher, or coach, when you point the finger of blame remember that three fingers are pointing back at you. So before you start off by blaming somebody else for a problem that has occurred, you may want to take a look at yourself first.

CHAPTER 33

Read

I've mentioned this earlier in Chapter 8, but I feel it is so important, I want to address this point again. The great author Og Mandino once wrote;

> *"The only difference from you now*
> *and you five years from now,*
> *are the people that you meet*
> *and the things that you read."*

This was a man who has sold millions of books. Some say he was the most widely read inspirational and self-help author in the world. I would take heed to his words. Life is too short for you to learn all there is to know by personal experience. Reading is an excellent way to shorten your learning curve. The gifts of knowledge, insight, and experience are all bestowed to us in the words they write; available to all, used by so few.

Make it a part of your daily routine to read something that will help you become a better person. *(at least 5 days per week)*

CHAPTER 34

The Future

John Schaar once wrote about the future in this manner.

"The future is not a result of choices among alternative paths offered by the present, but a place that is created first in mind and will, created next in activity. The future is not some place we are going to, but one we are creating. The paths to it are not found but made and the activity of making them changes both the maker and the destination."

In more simple words folks ... the way I look at it ...

If it is to be, it's up to me.

Go out there and make it a great one!

CHAPTER 35

Telling The Truth

THE ONLY WAY

The truth is but a simple thing,
for it knows no right or wrong.
There are those who would alter it,
to make the truth be gone.

They will speak, imply, suggest
what you know are not the facts.
But the truth will remain the same,
rest assured it will be back.

It may be for the moment,
the truth is not revealed.
There you stand betrayed by one,
accused of what's not real.

But for those of us who have been
wronged, take solace in what I say.
There will come a time where all will
know in some uncertain way.

The truth will rise above it all
and prove their words were wrong.
Causing those who spoke the words,
reputations now be gone.

The truth is but a simple thing,
it may be hard to say.
The truth is but a simple thing,
and for me the only way.

Robert Owen Stevenson

They can take everything away from you, your wealth, all your earthly possessions and even your health, but they cannot take away your integrity; only YOU can give that away.

And once you give it away you can never have it back. Once you lie to me, I know I can never trust you again. Once you steal from me I know I can never trust you again. I am not speaking of the actions of a child here. I am speaking about the actions of an adult who has the ability to make a choice.

My dad had a simple way of looking at the truth. He said; *"You'll never have to worry about remembering what you said, as long as you tell the truth. If someone asks you what happened for a second time, you don't have to try and remember what you said the first time, you just tell it like it is."*

The problem I see occurring over and over today in our society is that people are making the wrong choices where money is concerned. The power of the almighty dollar is amazing. And after they make the wrong choice, better themselves financially and then get caught, they just apologize and rationalize the truth away. They come up with excuses like:

◈ *"Everyone else was doing it, I was just the one who got caught."*
◈ *"It wasn't THAT wrong."*
◈ *"They've got millions so what I took will never be noticed."*
◈ *"I deserve it. For the little they pay me, it's only fair."*

Then, we the American public, forgive and forget, if it is advantageous for us to do so. The examples of this corruptness fill the pages of newspapers around the country. Here is an example of what I mean. Several years ago in the St. Petersburg Times they wrote an article about a former congressman who agreed to a plea bargain pleading guilty to two federal corruption charges and served

17 months in prison. Two years prior to this plea bargain agreement, this congressman's 17 felony counts centered on the misuse of his office. They included charges that he hired no-show employees, received kickbacks from workers, embezzled money from the U.S. Congressional House Post Office and used government money for personal and family expenses. Altogether, according to the indictment, the corruption involved more than $500,000.

But it all finally caught up with him. Washington's old boy network could not totally alter the truth this time. The judge who sentenced him was not a part of Washington's old boy network either. Judge Norma Holloway Johnson, a middle-aged black woman had that responsibility. On behalf of the American people, she chewed the congressman up one side and down the other before she packed him off to prison.

> St. Petersburg Times: The Honorable Judge said: *"When I think of your case, the one phrase that comes to my mind is betrayal of trust. You have brought a measure of disgrace on the institution you have had the privilege of serving for a number of years. You have shamelessly abused your power. The guilty pleas don't reflect the breadth of your crimes. In your important position, you capriciously pursued a course of personal gain for you, your family and your friends. You have stained them as well as yourself and the high position you held. The penalty your family will suffer will be the burden of conscience, will be the burden of disgrace that will always be associated with your tenure in Congress."*

He never apologized and he never explained. He even said that he hopes to re-enter public life when he gets out of prison. Now that is a scary thought, but he knows how the public mind works. He knows people forget … at least some people that is. I know one who won't.

_____

Abraham Lincoln said:

"I am bound to win,

but I am bound to be true.

I am not bound to succeed,

but I am bound to live up to what I have.

I must stand with anybody that stands right

and part company with him when he goes wrong."

_____

> **_"If you lose your wealth, you have lost nothing._**
> **_If you lose your health, you have lost something._**
> **_But if you lose your integrity, everything is lost."_**
>
> **Patrick Brosnan**

Thomas Jefferson's Philosophy

In matters of principle, stand like a rock,
in matters of taste, swim with the current.

Give up money, give up fame, give up science,
give the earth itself and all it contains,
rather than do an immoral act.

And never suppose, that in any possible situation,
or under any circumstances,
it is best for you to do a dishonorable thing,
though it can never be known but to appear to you.

Whenever you are to do a thing,
though it can never be known but to yourself,
ask yourself how you would act were all the world looking at you,
and act accordingly.

He who permits himself to tell a lie once,
finds it much easier to do it a second and third time,
till at length it becomes habitual:
He tells a lie without attending to it,
And truths without the world's believing him.

In the movie *Rob Roy*, the children of Rob Roy ask their father, *"What is Honor."* His response was, *"Honor is what you give to yourself."*

To my son I say:

Honesty, Integrity, Honor can never be taken away, only given up.

So guard them dearly, for once given up, they can never be returned.

Eagles Do This
Turkeys Don't

CHAPTER 36

WASIMS

Beware of those *desktop managers;* those who feel safe only in their offices, or those that think they know the best way to do it, because they did it that way *10 years ago*. In preparing for one of my programs I was fortunate to interview a young lady concerning the causes of stress in the workplace. She told me about a program they had implemented within her company that made a lot of sense in reducing stress in their work environment. They called it *WASIMS - Work A Shift In My Shoes.* This young lady worked in the MIS (*Management Information Systems*) department for a major Fortune 50 company. She explained that in order for their management staff to make good decisions they needed certain information. Much of that information came from computers being handled by personnel who have a customer standing right in front of them while this data was being entered. She said, *"We don't design a new system or procedure and put it in place, making it standard operating procedure, until those designing the system come Work A Shift In Our (My) Shoes."*

Hey folks ... what management wants, what your people can provide, and what the client will allow, may all be different. For those managers out there setting policy, making changes, implementing procedures ... do yourself, your company, and especially your people a favor. Get out there doing their job, asking questions, and finding out *today's environment*. Don't brashly request something today you are probably going to regret later. Go **Work A Shift In <u>Their</u> (My) Shoes.** Not only will you learn something, you'll gain their respect as well.

CHAPTER 37

Teamwork

Together **E**verybody **A**chieves **M**ore

It may sound corny but it's true. The power of teamwork is incredible. You've heard it said, *The chain is only as strong as it's weakest link.* Well, the same principle applies to companies as well.

It's the weak link in a company that is going to cost it business. It only takes one person to turn a customer totally against a company. And when the customer leaves, they don't say *Bill, or Mary or John did a lousy job* ... they say the name of the company.

Think about all the times you have received lousy service and decided never to deal with that company again. How many people in that organization caused you to take your business elsewhere. The majority of the time, the answer is one person.

Companies can spend millions of dollars in advertising to get you to try them out, and in a blink of an eye, you're never coming back because of *Bill, or Mary or John.*

I think the following example of a typewriter having every key working perfectly except one, really puts in perspective the power and importance of teamwork.

XVXRY KXY MUST WORK

Xvxn though my typxwritxr is an old modxl it doxs work quitx wxll xxcxpt for onx of thx kxys. I wishxd many timxs that it workxd pxrfxctly. It is trux that thxrx arx forty-onx kxys that function wxll xnough, but just onx kxy not working makxs thx diffxrxncx.

Somxtimxs it may sxxm that in an organization, thx onx or onxs wx arx concxrnxd with, arx somxwhat likx my typxwritxr - not all thx pxoplx arx working propxrly. You may say to yoursxlf, "Wxll, I am only onx pxrson. I won't makx a diffxrxncx bxcausx any program to bx xffxctivx nxxds thx activx participation of xvxry mxmbxr."

So thx nxxt timx you think you arx only onx pxrson and that your xfforts arx not nxxdxd, rxmxmbxr my typxwritxr and say to yoursxlf,

"*I am a kxy mxmber of my organization,
and I am nxxdxd vxry much.*

Anon.

The reputation
of any company
can be affected
by just one person.

"Do We Have As Much Sense As A Goose?"

This spring when you see geese heading back north for the summer flying along in a "V" formation, you might be interested in knowing what scientists have discovered about why they fly that way. It has been learned that as each bird flaps its wings, it creates an uplift for the bird immediately following.

By flying in a "V" formation, the whole flock adds at least 71% greater flying range than if each bird flew on its own.

Basic Truth #1: *People who share a common direction and sense of community can get where they are going quicker and easier because they are traveling on the thrust of one another.*

Whenever a goose falls out of formation, it suddenly feels the drag and resistance of trying to go it alone and quickly gets back into formation to take advantage of the lifting power of the bird immediately in front.

Basic Truth #2: *If we have as much sense as a goose, we will stay in formation with those who are headed the same way we are going.*

When the lead goose gets tired, he rotates back in the wing and another goose flies point.

Basic Truth #3: *It pays to take turns doing hard jobs with people or with geese flying north.*

The geese honk from behind to encourage those up front to keep up their speed.

Basic Truth #4: *We need to be careful what we say when we honk from behind.*

Finally, when a goose gets sick or is wounded by gun shots and falls out, two geese fall out of formation and follow him down to help and protect him. They stay with him until he is either able to fly or until he is dead, and then they launch out on their own or with another formation to catch up with their group.

Anon.

The Final Truth

Together you stand, divided you fall.

It takes no more than the sense of a goose to understand the importance of standing by each other.

CHAPTER 38

Leadership

"Of the best leader, when he is gone, they will say:
We did it ourselves."

Chinese Proverb

Many people profess to have it, that *Leadership Ability,* but few people truly possess it. They read the books, listen to the tapes, go to the seminars, and then pronounce themselves **Leaders.** They use words like *empowerment, total quality management, excellence, vision, commitment,* and in the same breath, want to take the credit. As James O'Toole, a professor and leadership expert puts it, **"Ninety-five percent of American managers today say the right thing. Five percent actually do it."**

I recently worked with an old friend who had chosen to go with a new company. Having worked with him several times before in other organizations, I had seen his management style in action. It was a shear delight to watch him operate in an entirely new company, with all new people, and see that he had already been awarded the title of LEADER by his people: a man who respects, understands, directs, motivates, and helps his people; a man who can be given a difficult task and accomplish it while at the same time CARING for his people and customers; **a *man who understands that great leadership will seem like less leadership.***

It is not how your people perform when you are there, but how they perform when you are not, that is the benchmark of a true leader.

The superior leader
gets things done with little motion.
He imparts instructions not through
many words but through a few deeds.
He keeps informed about everything
but interferes hardly at all.
He is a catalyst, and though things
would not get done as well
if he weren't there,
when they succeed he takes no credit.
And because he takes no credit,
credit never leaves him.

LAO-TZU

We all need to take responsibility
for those who follow us.

Do it not to be thanked.

Do it not to take the credit.

Do it because
you want to
and as a
gesture of
repayment
for those who
have done it
for you.

Robert Stevenson

Section IV

The Personal Side of The Game

CHAPTER 39

Let The People You Love — Know It

Don't let the words go unsaid. Don't put off that loving touch until tomorrow. Don't put off sending that note, or flowers, or card. Don't let your daily routine be the killer of romance in your life. Don't let familiarity, *the...oh they know I love them attitude,* set in on you.

If today was the last day of your life ...

How would you live it?
Who would you call to tell them you love them?
Who would you want to hold, hug or kiss.

We all have a tendency to get so caught up with our daily routine, pressures at work, *things-to-do* lists, that the people we love sometimes end up taking second place. If you are doing all these things because of the people you love, doesn't it make a little sense to put a little love in your daily routine, too.

The GOTTA DO'S seem to always get in the way. I *Gotta Do* this or I *Gotta Do* that, and with all these *Gotta Do's* I just don't have time for a little love and affection today; they'll understand.

I remember when I was dating my wife Annie. I still had a huge list of *Gotta Do's* but I always figured out a way to be with her. Isn't it amazing what hormones, lust, passion can do for a list of *Gotta Do's*; it kind-of makes them just evaporate, go away, and seem not so important.

Put **Tell-Em You Love Them** at the top of your *Gotta Do* list. It will do wonders for you as well as those you love.

> *Let them know you care,*
> *because someday*
> *you won't have a tomorrow*
> *to tell them,*
> *and you'll never know*
> *when that someday is.*

Eagles Do This
Turkeys Don't

CHAPTER 40

Friends

Make new friends, but keep the old;

Those are silver, these are gold.

New-made friendships, like new wine,

Age will mellow and refine.

Friendships that have stood the test –

Time and change — are surely best;

Brow and wrinkle, hair grow gray;

Friendship never knows decay.

For 'mid old friends, tried and true,

Once more we our youth renew.

But old friends, alas! may die;

New friends must their place supply.

Cherish friendship in your breast –

New is good, but old is best;

Make new friends, but keep the old;

Those are silver, these are gold.

Anon.

A person with who you dare to be yourself.

Frank Crane

One who knows all about you and loves you just the same.

Elbert Hubbard

One who has the same enemies as you do.

Abraham Lincoln

A true friend unbosoms freely, advises justly, assists readily, adventures boldly, takes all patiently, defends courageously, and continues a friend unchangeably.

William Penn

One who excuses you when you have made a fool of yourself.

Anon.

One who is here today and here tomorrow.

Anon.

One who walks in when the rest of the world walks out.

Anon.

A true friend is someone you can count on.

Robert Owen Stevenson

Refer to Chapter 44 - What Are They Really Saying About You - Page 192, 2nd paragraph from the bottom: *"I can't say that I have lots of friends ..."*

CHAPTER 41

Serenity Prayer

GOD grant me the power

to accept the things

I cannot change,

the courage to change

the things that I can,

and the wisdom

to know the difference.

Anon.

CHAPTER 42

Christmas

My Personal Christmas Letter to You

I love the holidays. Tradition to me is important; putting on Christmas ornaments that have been in the family for years and looking at the dates on them, trying to remember where we were and what we were doing.

I'll always remember my first Christmas with Annie. We were on a tight budget our first Christmas together so instead of spending money we didn't have on ornaments for the tree that wasn't up yet, she bought a do-it-yourself paint kit of 40 flat wooden Christmas figures. Annie hand painted every one, front and back, while I was on the road. I never knew she was doing it until she surprised me Christmas Eve with them.

Every year she suggests that we keep them off the tree because she says ... *"Rob, they are just cheap little ornaments"* ... but to me they can't be replaced. They hang there quietly among the fancy expensive ornaments, shining softly when the tree lights flicker, all with gentle smiles on their faces. You see, they know what they represent to me ... *giving, caring, loving, tradition, family and friends* ... they feel the love in my heart when I proudly display them at the front of the tree.

My wife, my son, my family, and friends, make my holiday season a joyous time for me. Know that you and yours are special to me and may your holidays be as happy as mine and filled with the meaning of 40 wooden figures.

The Value Of A Smile At Christmas

It costs nothing, but creates much.

It enriches those who receive, without impoverishing those who give.

It happens in a flash and the memory of it sometimes lasts forever.

None are so rich they can get along without it, and none so poor but are richer for its benefits.

It creates happiness in the home, fosters good will in a business, and its the countersign of friends.

It is rest to the weary, daylight to the discouraged, sunshine to the sad, and Nature's best antidote for trouble.

Yet it cannot be bought, begged, borrowed, or stolen, for it is something that is of no earthly good to anybody till it is given away.

And if in these few remaining days of this busy holiday season, one of our associates' should be too tired to give you a smile, may we ask you leave one of yours?

For nobody needs a smile so much as those who have none left to give.

Our hope is that you have many things to smile about over this holiday season.

Anon.

CHAPTER 43

Moms & Dads

My wife and I took on the job five years ago. We wanted the position, but had no idea, in our wildest dreams, what we were in for. Time, frustration, fear, and worry became the norm every day. They consume your time, drive you nuts, you're scared to death something is going to hurt them, and you worry yourself sick if you are doing the right thing. And then in an instant, they say three simple words, *"I love you,"* and everything else doesn't seem to matter.

We know we have a lot to learn in the *parent business* to qualify as great parents, but there is one thing our son knows without any doubt; we love him. We don't want him to ever worry about that. We feel that love can do more for his self-esteem, motivation, desire, and achievement than anything else. So ...

Teach them	Scold them
Help them	Show them
Correct them	Applaud them
Console them	Play with them
Laugh with them	Pray with them

But most of all ... LOVE THEM.

A Gift for Dad

I walked into the kitchen today,
no special day it was.
My son was playing with his toys
as he usually always does.
He stopped and turned and said to me,
"I need a hug and a kiss."
I knelt to comply with his request
for this was something I wouldn't want to miss.

But he added to this special moment
with such simple words to say.
He stopped and smiled and said to me,
on this seemingly uneventful day.
"I love you Dad," and he smiled again,
then skipped on back to play.

I know the day will come too soon,
when he will be on his own.
So God entrusted him with this *Gift*
to insure I'd never be alone.

I spoke to my Dad today,
we chatted for awhile.
I paused to say, *"I love you Dad,"*
And could feel the *Gift* in his smile.

Robert Owen Stevenson

My Influence

A careful man I ought to be;
A little fellow follows me.

I dare not go astray,
For fear he'll go the selfsame way.

Not once can I escape his eyes;
Whate'er he sees me do, he tries.

Like me he says he's going to be—
That little chap who follows me.

He thinks that I am good and fine;
Believes in every word of mine.

The base in me he must not see,
The little chap who follows me.

I must remember as I go,
Through summer sun and winter snow;

I'm building for the years to be,
That little chap who follows me.

Author Unknown

There is one time in my life that I am satisfied with second place; and that is in being a parent. My wife Annie never ceases to amaze me in her patience with our son. She never forgets anything when it comes to him. I watched her carry him for nine months and then give birth to him, and it is there, that I believe makes the difference. I don't know how to explain it, but it is beautiful to witness. I am not saying that she loves him anymore than I do, but something special is there. As I said, I see it, I can't explain it, and I never want to replace it.

God was very unfair in this child bearing program as far as the sharing of the discomfort, change in physical appearance, PAIN. But, then again, I know for a fact, that the great mothers would have it no other way. It's that *something special closeness* they have with their children, over we fathers, that makes it all worth while. Yes I must say, second place is just fine for me.

God could not be everywhere so he therefore made mothers.
Jewish Proverb

*And for you Moms out there
that are doing both jobs,
God has a special place in heaven for you.*

CHAPTER 44

What Are They Really Saying About You

What's your name? Not your legal name given to you by your parents ... but your real name ... the one people hang on you. As you go through life, people hang nicknames on you ... many of them may represent some crazy thing you did when you were young. Paul "Bear" Bryant, the famous football coach from the University of Alabama, got the nickname Bear because he wrestled a bear at the county fair. I don't know if he won the match, but the nickname stayed with him all his life. That's what people called him.

I've had a few nicknames in my time, but there was one I wasn't really fond of. In ninth grade my mother wanted to give me a surprise birthday party ... so she showed up at football practice, with all the fixings for a birthday party in the car. Cake, soft drinks, you name it, she had it. During the festivities, there was an unfortunate occurrence; a word that was uttered by my Mom, in front of the entire football team. It was an innocent word. A *nickname* that had been spoken in the "Privacy" of our home often, but this was not a public word.

Mom needed me to get something else out of the car, and she asked me by saying, *"Precious, would you go get the Cokes in the trunk."* At that moment, time froze for me. The party stopped. Not a soul had missed the word. Before the word had been spoken, I was the quarterback, the captain of the football team. From that point on, I was *Precious*. It didn't matter where I was that year, the name stuck. On the football field, basketball court, running track or in the classroom, I was now *Precious*.

My Dad was in the military and as it is in the military you move often. Dad got a new assignment and we had to move that summer. Thank God.

Over thirty years later, *Precious* appeared again. At a dinner party with some very close friends my wife shared the story of *Precious* and everyone got a great laugh, me included. Then the next day I was to play in a tennis tournament with Dave Middleton, a very close friend of mine, who also happened to be in attendance at the dinner party. As I approached the clubhouse, I heard a huge roaring voice exclaim, *"Precious ... we're on court four."* Time froze, all tennis play ceased and the entire club turned to see who *Precious* was. There I stood, identified again as the infamous *Precious*. So what did I do. I said, *"Coming Sweetheart"* ... and kept walking. Now Dave is 6'6" and weighs about 240 and I'm not exactly a little guy ... so there may have been thoughts or comments ... but most were contained.

So here I stand before you, *Precious, also known by other aliases of Robin Hood, Scooter, and Preacher* ... but those explanations are for another time. It's nice to have nicknames. It's even nicer to remember how you acquired them. But those are the names that are spoken in front of you. What is really important is what nicknames are being spoken behind your back.

I can't say that I have lots of friends. To me, this is a term that is used too loosely these days. I do know a lot of people, but classifying them as a friend, now that's something very special in my opinion.

Remember Dave, we've been friends for years. We played tennis together for over ten years, seeing each other about every week.

Then there was a long period of time that we didn't see each other for months. But if I ever needed anything, I knew I could always call on him. If I told him a secret, it never went any further. If I called and asked for advice, he always had the time. If I needed to borrow something, it was as if I owned it. Words that describe him are successful, dependable, confident but humble, educated but also wise, funny, happy, tolerant.

I could entrust him with my home, my money, my family and never worry for a moment. If I called him at 3 o'clock in the morning and said I needed to see him, he would be there. There are many nicknames I could hang on him ... the funny silly ones, that represents a special moment in our lives ... but he knows as do I ... the one that matters most ... is being called my *friend*.

What do people say about you behind your back?

Party Animal	Attila the Hun
Know-It-All but Never-Does	Arrogant
Lazy	Drinking King
Just Gets By	Always Late
Never Hits The Hip	TURKEY

You know I've never met a successful "PARTY ANIMAL." I've known lots of them, but they never seemed to be the real successful ones. I've also found that the people who boast the most are the ones who are the most insecure.

You might want to write down a list of how you would like to be described behind your back. This is a simple exercise. Now, start living your life so that is what they will be saying. Think, write, implement, succeed.

CHAPTER 45

Egos

*Conceit is a disease that effects everyone
except the person who has it.*

I don't know who said that, but it sure is true. On the other hand, you have to have confidence. Sometimes you can walk a fine line between conceit and confidence but never throw in boastful arrogance. Arrogance is something we can all do without.

Talking about yourself is a sure way to not succeed; most people out there, don't care. Keep your victories, accomplishments, successes to yourself. When asked about them, be brief, to-the-point, and humble.

The way you display your ego can be a major deterrent in the success you claim in life. The best way for someone to find out how great you are, is for them to find out from anybody other than you.

When your ego engages your mind, your intellect disengages When your intellect disengages, problems start to occur. Therefore, large egos can be a very expensive trait to possess. The reality is folks, that if today you are the fastest person on earth, there will soon be somebody faster. If you're the strongest, there will soon be somebody stronger. If you're the greatest, Realtor, broker, lawyer, doctor, or artist, there will soon be somebody better.

I once heard it said that an *Egotist is one who talks about himself so much that he gives you no time to talk about yourself. A self-made man who worships their creator.* These are not flattering words.

One sure way to keep your ego in check is to make sure you do less than half the talking. And when you do speak, don't dwell on you; you already know you.

I know some very wealthy people who have huge egos and are a pain to be around. They have it all, know it all and want you to know it. But they really don't have it all; respected, honored, revered, adored, valued and appreciated they are not. They think they have a lot of friends, but if the truth be known, they have few. Life is too short to be socializing with the likes of them.

If you want to be liked, then get interested in other people. Don't worry, there are lots of hours in the day, when you are by yourself, that you can love yourself.

Remember;

A mind that is full of itself will never learn.

Chapter 46

Principles For
A Well-Balanced Life

The great German philosopher Goethe laid out the following principles for leading a well-balanced life.

> *Health enough to make work a pleasure.*
> *Wealth enough to support your needs.*
> *Strength enough to battle difficulties*
> *and overcome them.*
> *Patience enough to toil until some good*
> *has been accomplished.*
> *Grace enough to confess your sins*
> *and forsake them.*
> *Charity enough to see the good*
> *in your neighbors.*
> *Love enough to move you to be useful*
> *and helpful to others.*
> *Faith enough to make real the things of God.*
> *Hope enough to remove all fears*
> *concerning the future.*

Or you may want to give consideration to The Barnes Creed. Mr. Barnes was the business partner to Thomas A. Edison.

The Barnes Creed

1. I will channel my mind toward prosperity and success by keeping my thoughts as much as possible on the major goal I have set for myself.
2. I will free my mind of self-made limitations by drawing on the power of the Creator through unlimited faith.
3. I will keep my mind free of greed and covetousness by sharing my blessings with those who are worthy to receive them.
4. I will substitute a positive type of discontent for indolent self-satisfaction so that I may continue to learn and grow both physically and spiritually.
5. I will keep an open mind on all subjects and toward all people so that I may rise above intolerance.
6. I will look for good in others and school myself to deal gently with their faults.
7. I will avoid self-pity. Under all circumstances I will seek stimulation to greater effort.
8. I will recognize and respect the difference between the material things I need and desire, and my rights to receive them.
9. I will cultivate the habit of "going the extra mile" and always rendering more and better service than is expected of me.
10. I will turn adversity and defeat into assets by remembering that they always carry with them the seed of equivalent benefits.
11. I will always conduct myself toward others in such a manner that I may never be ashamed to face the man I greet at the mirror in the morning.
12. Finally, my daily prayer will be for wisdom to recognize and live my life in harmony with the overall purpose of the Creator.

These are simple words to read but difficult principles to follow. I would suggest you make a copy of each list and tape one to the mirror in your bathroom. Every time you brush your teeth or brush your hair, read it. Do this for thirty days and then replace that list with the second list and keep it there for thirty days. In two short months Goethe's and Barne's creeds for living a well balanced life will become a part of you.

When you want to build a house, before your ever stick a stake in the ground you start with a blueprint. If you want to build the house right, you stick to the blueprint. The same is true with leading a well-balanced life. You need a blueprint of some kind to follow. Many of us do this subconsciously, based on the input from our parents, teachers, coaches and friends. I feel you will be better served if you decide upon "YOUR CREED" and make it become reality.

I would like to give emphasis to one major point that both creeds address, but do so in somewhat of an indirect manner. *Do unto others as you would have them do unto you.* Think of all the problems in the world that would be solved if we all followed those simple words. Most all of us were taught *The Golden Rule* in grade school, but when you read the newspapers today or watch the news on television, it becomes all too evident that it isn't being practiced by everyone. The rule is becoming more the exception than the norm.

Many times I deal with those who practice the rule of; *Do unto others for your sole benefit and then bug out.* The WII-FM people — **What's In It - For Me.** So many people today are driven by money, power, and prestige and nothing else. You've heard the expressions;

"He'd sell out his mother for a buck."

"If he was in a life boat with his parents and there was only enough water for one person to survive, he would be thinking of how to spell the word orphan."

"She thinks a Win-Win negotiation means that she beat you twice."

You need your health to enjoy your wealth and you need your family and friends to enjoy it all. Balance your life and smell the roses. Our objective here is to live a *successful well-balanced life*. Let's address the issue of success.

<u>SUCCESS</u>

Success is speaking words of praise,
In cheering other people's ways,
In doing just the best you can,
With every task and every plan,
It's silence when your speech would hurt,
Politeness when your neighbor's curt,
It's deafness when scandal flows,
And sympathy with others' woes,
It's loyalty when duty calls,
It's courage when disaster falls,
It's patience when the hours are long,
It's found in laughter and in song,
It's in the silent time or prayer,
In happiness and in despair,
In all of life and nothing less,
We find this thing we call success.

Author Unknown

More and more people are basing success solely on materialistic possessions; *the one who dies with the most toys wins.* I don't know if you are aware of how much money billionaire Howard Hughes left behind when he died; he left *All Of It.*

I want money for the freedom it brings with it. I want possessions for the comforts they include. But to have those at the expense of my health, loss of my family and destruction of friendships, makes none of it worthwhile.

Golden Rules For Living

If you open it, close it.
If you turn it on, turn it off.
If you unlock it, lock it up.
If you break it, admit it.
If you can't fix it, call in someone who can.
If you borrow it, return it.
If you value it, take care of it.
If you move it, put it back.
If it belongs to someone else and you want to use it, get
    permission.
If you don't know how to operate it, leave it alone.
If it's none of your business, don't ask questions.
If it aint' broke, don't fix it.
If it will brighten someone's day, say it.
If it will tarnish someone's reputation, keep it to yourself.

Author Unknown

To give closure to our formula for a well-balanced life I feel we need the words of George Eliot.

Count That Day Lost

If you sit down at set of sun

And count the acts that you have done,

And, counting, find

One self-denying deed, one word

That eased the heart of him who heard,

One glance most kind

That fell like sunshine where it went —

Then you may count that day well spent.

But if, through all the livelong day,

You've cheered no heart, by yea or nay —

If, through it all

You've nothing done that you can trace

That brought the sunshine to one face —

No act most small

That helped some soul and nothing cost —

Then count that day as worse than lost.

Chapter 47

Making A Difference

One day a man was walking along the seashore. He noticed that during the night many seashells and starfish had washed upon the shore. Thoroughly enjoying the morning sun and cool sea air, the man strolled for miles along the sand.

Far off in the distance, he saw a small figure dancing. The man was joyous that someone was celebrating life in such a grand and uninhibited manner. As he drew closer, however, it became apparent that perhaps the figure was not dancing, but perhaps repeatedly performing some ritual.

*Approaching the small figure, the man noticed that it was a child. The girl was methodically picking up starfish from the shore and tossing them back into the surf. The man paused for a moment, puzzled, then asked, "**Why are you throwing those starfish?**"*

*"**If I leave these starfish on the beach,**" she replied, "**the sun will dry them, and they will die. So I'm throwing them back into the ocean because I want them to live.**"*

*The man was thoughtful for a moment, impressed with the child's thoughtfulness. Then he motioned up and down the miles and miles of beach and said, "**There must be millions of starfish along here! How can you possibly expect to make a difference?**"*

The girl pondered the man's words for a moment, then she slowly leaned over, reached down, and carefully picked up another starfish from the sand. Pulling back, she arched the starfish gently into the surf.

She turned to the man and smiled, **"You may be right,"** *she said,* **"but I made a difference for that one!"**

Anon.

Have you helped any Starfish (the human kind that is) lately?

> *If you're going through life just in it for you, then you really aren't living, you're just passing through.*
>
> **Robert Owen Stevenson**

Epilogue

"If"

If you can keep your head when all about you
Are losing theirs and blaming it on you;
If you can trust yourself when all men doubt you,
And make allowance for their doubting too.
If you can wait and not be tired of waiting,
Or be lied about, don't deal in lies,
Or be hated, and not take to hating,
And yet don't look too good, nor talk too wise.
If you can dream and make dreams your master;
If you can think and not make thoughts your aim,
If you can meet with Triumph and Disaster
And treat those two impostors just the same;
If you can bear to hear the truth you've spoken
Twisted by knaves to make a trap for fools,
Or watch the thing you gave your life to, broken,
And stoop and build them up with worn out tools.
If you can make one heap of all your winnings
And risk it on one turn of pitch-and-toss,
And lose, and start again at your beginnings
And never breathe a word about your loss;
If you can force your heart and nerve and sinew
To serve your turn long after they are gone,
And so hold on when there is nothing left you
Except the will which says to them: *"Hold on!"*
If you can talk with crowds and not lose your virtue,
Or walk with Kings — nor lose the common touch,
If neither foes nor loving friends can hurt you,
If all men count with you, but none too much;
If you can fill the unforgiving minute
With sixty seconds' worth of distance to run,
Yours is the Earth and everything that's in it,
And - which is more - you'll be a Man, my son!

Rudyard Kipling

I think Mr. Kipling's poem and the following quote by Aristotle bring excellent closure to our time together.

> # We are what we repeatedly do.
>
> # Excellence, then, is not an act, but a habit.
>
> Aristotle

Just remember,

the "*If*" is up to you and you alone.

Good Luck
and
Always Keep

SEEKING EXCELLENCE.

More Turkey Examples

(Continued from Introduction)

11. A person who has more than 10 items in the *10 Items or Less Line*.

12. People / Schools / Associations / Clubs ...etc. who tell you that certain requirements must be met for you to qualify, join, be accepted ... but someone else gets in because of who they know.

13. Bosses who would never do what they require you to do.

14. Parents who expect their children not to do what they do.

15. A person who dings your car door.

16. People who always seem to be complaining. (I call them *"Professional Depressions"*)

17. A person who isn't handicapped but gets a handicapped parking sticker just to get better parking.

18. A policeman who gives you a ticket for driving 38 in a 35 m.p.h. zone.

19. People who give you their car insurance information at the scene of an accident knowing it has been cancelled.

20. A person who cuts in line.

21. Bosses who manage by fear.

22. Employees who steal from their company.

23. Neighbors who borrow things and then never bring them back.

24. People who sell you something knowing it is broken or will soon break.

25. People who start false rumors.

26. People who carry more than two bags on an airplane. (A purse or laptop don't count)

27. People who deface property for whatever the reason.

28. Stockbrokers/Financial Advisers who think of their commission first.

29. Salespeople who aren't knowledgeable about the product or service they are selling.

30. People who lie.

31. People who say it is ... when it really isn't. (the *out-of-context* quotes)

32. Reporters who tell you *"this is off the record"* and then print what you said.

33. People who want to succeed at your expense.

34. Bosses/Management personnel who never praise you. (that's what we pay them for - why should we have to praise them too?)

35. People who cheat to win.

36. Parents who won't wipe their child's running nose.

37. Car mechanics who tell you it's broken when it isn't and then charge you to fix it.

38. A spouse who forgets your birthday or anniversary.

39. A child who forgets their parents birthday.

40. Brown-nosers

41. People who act like they are better than you.

42. People who abuse their position of authority.

43. People who complain about being overweight when there is something they can do about it.

44. Friends who take advantage of your friendship.

45. People who keep you waiting, and waiting, and waiting.

46. Airline personnel who never tell what is really going on.

47. People who speak to you but keep their headsets on.

48. Parents who let their children run wild, disturbing others.

49. People who get in the right turn lane and go straight.

50. People who go 45 in a 55 m.p.h. zone.

51. People who go 54 or less on a 55 m.p.h. superhighway and stay in the left (passing) lane.

52. People who demand excellent service but tip poorly.

53. Coaches who use intimidation to motivate.

54. Parents who don't know where their children are.

55. People who talk in movie theaters during the movie.

56. People who wear hats in movie theaters.

57. Parents/Child Care Helpers who let a baby stay in a soiled diaper.

58. People who wear too much perfume/cologne.

59. Companies/people who pay the fine but admit no wrong/fault.

60. Judges who allow companies/people to pay the fine but admit no wrong/fault.

61. Noisy neighbors.

62. Relatives who show up unexpectedly.

63. Relatives who stay too long.

64. Relatives who visit you when they are on vacation, expecting you to act like you're on vacation, when you are working.

65. People who allow their children to do things in your home that they would never allow done in their home.

66. People who drive with their lights on bright as they approach your car.

67. People who ride your bumper especially when you have absolutely no chance of getting out of their way.

68. People who drive in the emergency lane to get ahead in traffic and then expect you to let them merge back in.

69. Grocery stores who re-label/re-date old meat.

70. Grocery stores who hide the bad fruit in the middle of the container.

71. Grocery stores who take the *out-of-date* meat and produce and sell it in their deli as fresh food for meals.

72. People who let their pets defecate in your yard rather than their own.

73. People who don't flush.

74. People who eat at shopping malls in the food court and leave their mess on the table.

75. Parents who are *Must Win Fanatics* at Little League sporting events.

76. A client who says *"the check is in the mail,"* when it isn't.

77. An employee who claims they hurt themselves on the job when they didn't, just to draw workman's compensation.

78. A person who collects unemployment insurance but never tries to get employed.

79. An athlete who tries to seriously injure another athlete with a *cheap shot*.

80. People who smoke in non-smoking areas.

81. Smokers who just put their cigarettes out anywhere they please.

82. An actor accepting an award who makes a political statement in their acceptance speech.

83. Companies who install a Voice Mail system that requires you to have a Ph.D. to understand or use it.

84. Politicians who won't balance the budget.

85. A politician who would spend thousands of tax payers dollars for personal Halloween costumes for him and his spouse.

86. Politicians who use government money for personal expenses, personal travel and vacations.

For those of you who have some *Turkey* examples
you would like to share in my next edition:

Please email them to:

info@robertstevenson.org

Please include a statement requesting submission in our next edition along with your consent releasing all rights for your original material.

INDEX

Robert Stevenson is President of Seeking Excellence, Inc.; a seminar and training company dedicated to assisting individuals and organizations in achieving their full potential. Mr. Stevenson conducts over 100 customized programs annually for corporations, associations, annual meetings and conventions, all designed to meet the specific needs of his clients.

His client list reads like a *Who's Who* in business; companies like Time Warner, Anheuser Busch, Prudential, Lockheed Martin, Fed Ex, Radio Shack, American Express, Blue Cross Blue Shield, ChevronTexaco, and HBO continue to rely on him for a fresh, unique perspective on businesses' most crucial issues. He has shared the podium with such renowned professionals as Tom Peters, former President George Bush, Anthony Robbins, General Norman Schwarzkopf, and Stephen Covey. If you are interested in receiving information about one or more of Mr. Stevenson's programs please contact:

SEEKING EXCELLENCE
A Robert Stevenson Corporation

Tel: (727) 781-4000 • Fax: (727) 789-5650
E-Mail: info@robertstevenson.org

We will be happy to provide you a complete media package that will include program descriptions, fees, scheduling and transportation requirements, along with a video highlight tape of Mr. Stevenson in action. This is an invitation to commit to a higher level of performance. We look forward to hearing from you.

www.robertstevenson.org

Seeking Excellence is a continuous journey where we should learn from the past, deal with the present, prepare for the future and appreciate it all.

Robert Stevenson